Diane
Gaudynski

GUIDE
to
MACHINE
QUILTING

American Quilter's Society
P. O. Box 3290 • Paducah, KY 42002-3290
www.AQSquilt.com

Located in Paducah, Kentucky, the American Quilter's Society (AQS) is dedicated to promoting the accomplishments of today's quilters. Through its publications and events, AQS strives to honor today's quiltmakers and their work and to inspire future creativity and innovation in quiltmaking.

EDITOR: BARBARA SMITH
GRAPHIC DESIGN: ELAINE WILSON
COVER DESIGN: MICHAEL BUCKINGHAM
QUILT PHOTOGRAPHY: CHARLES R. LYNCH, UNLESS OTHERWISE STATED
HOW -TO PHOTOGRAPHY: DIANE GAUDYNSKI

Library of Congress Cataloging-in-Publication Data
Gaudynski, Diane.
    Guide to machine quilting / by Diane Gaudynski
       p. cm.
Includes bibliographical references.
    ISBN 1-57432-796-8
    1. Machine quilting.   I. Title.
    TT835 .G38 2002
    746.46--dc21
             2002009502

Additional copies of this book may be ordered from the American Quilter's Society, PO Box 3290, Paducah, KY 42002-3290, or on line at www.AQSquilt.com.

DEDICATION

For my grandmother, Ruth Sellers Woolson (1899–1962), a quilter who loved me when I was little, made quilts for me to sleep under, and who perhaps knows I am a quilter too.

My great-great-grandmother made this machine-quilted bib for my grandfather, Milton Woolson, when he was a baby in the early 1900s. PHOTO: DIANE GAUDYNSKI

ACKNOWLEDGMENTS

SPECIAL THANKS TO...

My mother, Erma Hinterberg, who taught me to sew;

My father, John Hinterberg, who taught me to do a job well;

My husband, Alan, for his enthusiasm and support;

My brother, Neil Hinterberg, who unlocked the mysteries of computers for me;

My sister, Helen Hinterberg, for introducing me to pieced patchwork;

My sister, Mary Schmidt, for her constant encouragement and support;

My brother, Jim Hinterberg, who first taught me about "mud" colors;

and

Harriet Hargrave, who showed me the way;

Debra Wagner, who inspired me with her incredible machine workmanship;

and Caryl Bryer Fallert for her glorious art quilts.

CONTENTS

Introduction 6

Part I.
A New Tradition 9
  MACHINE QUILTING OVERVIEW 10
  MACHINE QUILTING SYSTEM 12
  EQUIPMENT & SUPPLIES 14
    Machine Quilting Needles
    and Threads (table). 25
  FABRIC PREPARATION. 28
  BATTING CHOICE. 32
  BACKING FABRIC 35
  MARKING 39
  PIN BASTING 42
  QUILTING TECHNIQUE 44
  PLAN OF ATTACK. 47
  THREAD TENSION 50
  WALKING FOOT QUILTING 55
    Starting and Stopping 56
    Managing the Quilt. 57
      FREQUENT WALKING-FOOT
      QUESTIONS 61
  FREE-MOTION QUILTING 65
    Along Came Harriet 65
    Beginning Free-Motion 65
    Quilting a Marked Design 69
    Echo Quilting 73
    Continuous Curves 78
    Feather Designs 83
    Lines and Grids. 87
    Stippling. 89
      FREQUENT FREE-MOTION
      QUESTIONS 97
  QUILTING SAMPLES 100

FINISHING TIPS 102
  Squaring the Quilt. 102
  Binding the Edges 103
  Washing the Quilt 104
  Drying the Quilt 105

YOUR FIRST QUILT 108
PREVENTING PAIN AND FATIGUE 111

Part II.
Machine-Quilting Projects 113
  TRIP AROUND THE WORLD
    WALL QUILT 114
  LOG CABIN REVISITED 120
  BASKET QUILT 126

Quilting Samples 136
Bibliography 141
About the Author 143

INTRODUCTION

When I was a small girl, my mother would take our family shopping to a wonderful store called the Metropolitan, which carried dry goods and just about everything else you might want, from underwear to licorice. On the mezzanine, the fabric department displayed aisles and aisles of stacked flat goods: cottons, wools, rich corduroys for back-to-school, gauzy curtain material, and heavy upholstery. As a 10-year-old, I viewed the fabric edges at eye level, so I was able to see the interplay between the rich colors and the endless designs and patterns where, by happenstance, they were stacked together. It was heaven. I didn't know it then, but this array was calling out to the dormant quilter inside me, waiting to be discovered.

My grandmother was a quilter, and although I never saw her quilting, my sis-ters and I slept under beautiful scrap quilts, lovingly pieced and hand quilted for us. The first quilt I made, when I was a teenager, was for my youngest sister, Helen, who later, when she was 16, taught me the basics of piecing patchwork. This first quilt contained simple embroidered pictures of children holding kittens. My mother sent off the blocks to my grandma, who added bright teal-blue sashing and borders and then hand quilted it. The finished quilt was beautiful, but even so, I didn't get hooked then and waited many years until the 1970s for my interest in quilting to revive.

I have used sewing machines ever since my first toy hand-cranked model. I asked Santa for it when I realized that hand sewing clothes for my doll, Elizabeth, was definitely not for me. My first grown-up machine was a Singer treadle with opulent Egyptian gilded motifs, a beautiful wood cabinet, and a nifty little green velvet-lined box that held any attachment you could ever want. My parents bought it for me at the local church auction for $2. Sewing simple clothing for Helen and tops and shorts for myself showed me that sewing was fun, it accomplished something wonderful, and machines were fascinating.

For many years, I sewed constantly: clothing, evening wear, curtains, baby sleepers, bedspreads, whatever. I loved the hours spent at the machine, the smell and sound of it. It didn't occur to me that something so relaxing could be transferred to the art of quiltmaking, which was something I had always considered a hand craft.

My first quilts were machine pieced from templates because there were no rotary cutters. I tied the first few into comforters with big puffy batts, and we stayed cozy and warm under them during our cold winter nights. But deep inside, I wanted to make quilts that were so heavily quilted they looked embossed, like old tin ceilings. I made a simple Streak-of-Lightning scrap quilt with hand-quilted straight lines, but it took me more than a year to quilt it, and it wasn't very good when it was finished. Sadly, to me, it looked like it had been basted and was just ready for some serious quilting. This hand quilting was far too tedious and slow for me, plus it aggravated a painful neck injury.

The arrival of Harriet Hargrave's machine-quilting book sent me into a world of discovery, of joy, of completion. Finally, I could make quilts with the simplicity of my grandmother's everyday ones but with extensive machine quilting.

I still enjoy the beauty of fabrics, their richness and variety, and find that most quilters also respond in the same way to fabric and quilts, with their colors, textures, and styles. I hope this book will give you the inspiration and tools to complete your quilts faster and better, whether by hand or machine, so you can have the fulfillment of this creative art.

From my background in sewing clothing, I learned valuable skills for piecing and quilt construction that I will share with you. I have been machine quilting for many years now, and all the little steps in the progress I made from beginner to accomplished quilter are in this book for you to read, try, and make your own. I hope you will sit down in a comfy chair and actually read the text as well as pore over the photos. Even if you have a sewing machine you like, you may want to read the section on the sewing machine and what to look for in one. It may give you some insight into how yours can be improved with additions that might make all the difference for machine quilting.

In our busy lives, many of us have turned to machine quilting as a way to make more quilts or to make quilts at all. However, machine quilting need not be tension-producing, difficult, or sub-standard. A machine-quilted quilt is not necessarily inferior or sloppy, for machine quilting is simply a different way to create a beautiful quilt. The same care and effort is used in machine work as in the finest hand work. With the right machine quilting skills, even simple everyday quilts with straight-line quilting can be exquisite. You can combine everyday quilt tops with "Sunday-best quilting" to make quilts that sing.

OCTOBER MORNING, 81" x 81". This traditional Delectable Mountains pattern is embellished with original feather designs and trapunto. The colors were inspired by autumn – the delicate lilac sky every morning and evening contrasting with the deep rich tones of the turning leaves in the surrounding hills. (Quilted with nylon monofilament thread, Cotton Classic® batt. 2000 Bernina Award for Machine Workmanship at the AQS Quilt Show and part of the permanent MAQS collection.)

Part I

A New TRADITION

MACHINE QUILTING OVERVIEW

An interviewer once asked me why quilters were turning to machine quilting, and I thought "because it is so much fun." Then I realized that, for many, it isn't fun. It's simply a faster way to quilt all the tops that need to be finished. For me, it was the pleasure, along with the desire to finish many quilts and do them justice, that led me to become a machine quilter. The immediacy of machine quilting is also a plus. You can see a quilt top come to life quickly with either simple or intricate quilting.

When I've been asked what are the most important ingredients that go into making a good machine quilter, I've had to pause and really think. Is it the sewing machine? The coordination? The speed? The age of the quilter? The desire and motivation?

After teaching machine quilting techniques, as well as piecing techniques for many years, I've come to realize that those who succeed have two things in common:

GOOD MENTAL ATTITUDE, AND

CORRECT BODY POSITION.

Mental Attitude

A good machine quilter is *relaxed*. You need a positive outlook, a "let's see how this goes" attitude. You could also use a streak of sheer old-fashioned stubbornness. My first efforts at machine quilting were pathetic, yet I only wanted to do more. Rather than give up, I dug in my heels and kept on doing it.

If you are relaxed, warm, and loose, you will be able to quilt for hours and feel like you've been relaxing in a recliner with a good book and a cat purring in your lap.

Mental tension translates into tight muscles, which makes for aches and pains no matter how correct your set-up for quilting may be. In the past, I assumed that, with the correct set-up, there would be no aches and pains. Wrong! After quilting on my first sewing machine for eight years, I bought a new one and set it up exactly like the old one: same chair, same table height, same light, same place in my room even. I quilted for several hours, and the next day felt sore all over. I decided then that the soreness was caused by mental tension from learning to use a new sewing machine with a completely different feel and operation.

My solution was to quilt a queen-sized quilt on the new machine. Soon the aches went away as I became used to the machine.

Then, whenever I passed my sewing room, I felt eager to be quilting rather than nervous, imagining the new machine as overpowering and scary.

Body Position

You need a set-up for machine quilting that will allow your body to be in a comfortable, relaxed position (Fig. 1–1). You quilt

Fig. 1–1. The author at her machine.

with your hands and fingers, not with your arms. Many quilters use their arms to "scrub floors" to move the quilt under the needle. It's so much easier to get perfect stitches and good control if you can rest your arms and move the quilt only with your hands and finger tips. The finger tips have a concentration of nerve endings, providing you with the tools to move and manipulate the quilt in rhythm with your foot on the speed control. If you cover your finger tips with gloves or use a hoop, you are taking the most sensitive part of your body away from the process, the part that signals to your brain what's going on there under the needle.

MACHINE HEIGHT

Ideally, the sewing machine surface should be at a height that will allow you to sit with your elbows bent at a 90° angle to the floor. For me, just having a surface 30"

from the floor and an adjustable chair height makes all the difference. I can rest my forearms on the quilt or the sewing cabinet and have a comfortable body position.

CHAIR HEIGHT

If you use an extension table for the sewing machine, then raise the chair's height so you are more comfortable. Many times, the wrong chair height will put stress on your lower back. Your thighs should be at a 90° angle to the floor, and your feet should not dangle. Even if the height is only an inch or so off, you will experience those aches and pains.

FOOT CONTROL

The shape and style of the foot control are important. I use my right foot for my foot control because I am right-handed. My entire foot rests on the pedal. I don't have to hold my foot up, keeping it in an unnatural position. My left foot rests on a spoke of the base of my chair to raise it up about the same amount. This keeps my body in line, without putting pressure on my lower back. There are supports made of plexiglas to raise the free foot to the same position as the one on the foot control. If you have lower-back problems, this item is definitely worth trying.

Some foot controls can cause undue stress on your leg muscles and foot. Sometimes, after demonstrating on students' machines in workshops, I notice that the top of my foot aches the next day. The cause is a poorly designed foot control. When you try out a machine for purchase, this is one of the important things to investigate. See if your sewing machine dealer will let you borrow the machine you are considering, for a day or two.

Machine Quilting System

It is the selection and combination of certain elements *used together as a system* that give quilting stitches their consistency and beauty.

For example, most machine quilters use a cotton batt, but many do not wash their finished quilts. Or, the sewing machine might be top of the line, state of the art, but the stitches are uneven and erratic. Perfectly good thread might be used, but there are little knots on the back. All of these things can be improved by selecting the proper techniques, tools, and methods, all part of the machine quilting system I use.

If you've been machine quilting for a while, yet your work remains at the same level, it's time to change something. My system has been adjusted many times, and I still tweak it, depending on the needs of each project. All parts of the system need to be coordinated and be in good working order for the quilt to have the look and quality you want.

Machine quilting doesn't mean fast quilting all the time. It is one of the biggest ironies of machine quilting that we think of it as being so much faster than hand quilting. We don't realize that it is necessary to slow down, learn the technique, and become comfortable handling a quilt and moving it under a needle. Speed will gradually increase as your skill does. Even when you become very skilled, many types of machine quilting will still be done at a slower rate. You will have to learn to make every stitch count, make every stitch of good quality, just as in hand quilting.

Every quilter will quilt at a different rate. The best speed is what is comfortable for you so that you get good results and feel relaxed and confident. In my workshops, I have seen too many quilters who have had teachers insist that only a fast speed is allowed, and others whose teachers have said "go slow." The reality is a combination of all speeds, and finding a speed that is good for you. It's okay to go fast, and it's okay to go slow.

Don't agonize about your speed. In classes, students tend to look at how fast everyone else is going, but this only adds stress to the learning process. If you see someone going faster on the same design you are quilting, try her speed and see if it helps. If not, maybe she is the one who should be slowing down to match your speed.

My system of machine quilting includes the following elements:

• **Body position.** Pay attention to body position and comfort so your quilting skills are optimized and body pains are minimized.

• **Relax.** Enjoy the process, accept the results, and know that you will be better with the next project. Machine quilting is a learned skill, needing repetition and reinforcement.

• **Sewing machine.** Select one that gives you a good stitch quality, easy tension adjustment, machine quilting feet, and proper foot control for speed variations.

- **Throat plate.** Replacing a damaged throat plate or filing down burrs around the opening can improve free-motion quilting quality immensely.

- **Free-motion foot.** Use a good free-motion foot for your machine, one that gives you the best possible visibility. Even if you need to cut out the front of the foot, do it!

- **Table or cabinet.** Set the machine in a table or cabinet, at a level even with the surrounding surface. Don't set it on top of a table.

- **Lighting.** Use proper lighting. Sometimes that means turning off the sewing machine light or the overhead room light to get the best possible visibility for quilting. Add a directional table lamp.

- **Grain line.** Pay close attention to the grain line of the fabric for piecing and quilting. Quilt straight lines on the bias to avoid distortion.

- **Starch.** Use starch to stabilize the fabric for piecing and to allow the quilt to slide easily under the needle for quilting.

- **Batting.** Choose a flat, thin batt, preferably cotton, that will roll up and fit in the sewing machine. It needs to provide some degree of shrinkage to enhance the quilting designs and give them texture.

- **Needles.** Needles designated as "sharps" eliminate bobbin pop-ups or tension difficulties, and they leave as small a hole in the quilt as possible for the type of thread chosen. Use new, sharp needles for the best possible results.

- **Short stitch and fine thread.** It's important to use a fine thread, especially in the bobbin, and a short stitch length for this system.

- **Tension.** Adjust the top and bottom tension as needed to balance the stitch.

- **Cone-thread holder.** Use a metal cone thread holder for the top thread to insure even delivery, smoothly wound bobbins, and fewer snarls and loops.

- **Quilt support.** Make sure the quilt is supported all around so that its weight doesn't drag on the needle. If there is any drag, it will be difficult or impossible to sew even stitches.

- **Hands.** Get a good grip, using aids if necessary, such as hoops, gloves, pads, or hand cream. Move your hands evenly, smoothly, and slowly.

- **Machine speed.** Vary the speed of the machine for the different parts of quilting. It's not all one speed!

- **Securing stitches.** Start and stop stitching lines so they are secure, yet not noticeable.

- **Double stitching.** Learn to double-stitch, or backtrack, over a line of stitching to get to another area of the quilting design without cutting the thread.

- **Look ahead.** Practice looking ahead of the needle, even in double stitching.

- **Stabilize the quilt.** Use invisible grid quilting to stabilize the quilt before free-motion quilting.

- **Quilt sequentially.** To gain expertise in various techniques, do all the straight lines at one time, then all the designs motifs, then all the stippling, so each technique is repeated and learned.

- **Wash the quilt.** After you have put in the last stitch, wash the quilt and then block it while it is wet.

EQUIPMENT & SUPPLIES

It was a peaceful autumn afternoon, and I was learning to free-motion quilt with my old sewing machine. It was already a venerable 20 plus years old when I purchased it right out of college. I didn't realize it, but over the years, it had lost its ability to sew at slower speeds and went full speed all the time, once it got over that initial jerky start. For sewing clothing and piecing, it was fine. I knew its quirks and little ways, so I took a deep breath, counted to three while it thought about starting up, and held on to my quilt for dear life while it raced ahead.

I found myself holding my breath and biting my tongue. My total concentration on moving the quilt ahead of the racing machine made me completely oblivious to everything around me. Sometime later, when my husband arrived home, he found the house filled with smoke and me still quilting away in my basement sewing room. I stopped, took a deep breath and choked. Surprised by the smoke from the motor, I was even more astonished to find my shoe had melted to the foot control, which was burning hot and smoking, too!

I learned from this experience that old machines sometimes can't take the pressure and will break down when subjected to hours of machine quilting. I repaired mine with a new foot control, motor, and cord, which was under $100. Then I purchased a new machine and never used the old one again, even though it had been my trusty companion for many years.

For today's machine quilter, the choices in machines, supplies, cabinets, and lights are daunting. When I began machine quilting, I needed only my old machine in a simple cabinet, bicycle clips, office clamps, safety pins, a walking foot, and a cotton batt. Options were limited. Now, there are many brands and styles of all of the products you need for machine quilting, and it's difficult to know which ones to choose.

EXPERIENCE WILL BE YOUR TEACHER:

• **Try a product** to see if it works and if you like it.

• **Don't keep using** something because you have always used it. Change can be good.

• **Ask friends,** be inquisitive in classes, ask quilters you respect what they use.

• **The most important** thing to select is the sewing machine itself.

The Sewing Machine

Choosing a sewing machine can be a confusing experience, and it is an expensive all-important tool that you will use every day and keep for years. Usually I tell students to buy from a dealer in their area who has a good reputation and a quality brand machine to sell. Many of the older models work fine, but whether you are selecting a used machine or a new one, there are a few crucial things to look for:

SPEED CONTROL

Be sure the foot control works well and is not too touchy, thereby creating sudden changes in speed. The machine should be slow and steady, and you should be able to sew one stitch at a time by using the foot control, not just by turning the hand wheel.

Make sure the machine has plenty of speed, especially if you are a quilter who really likes to burn rubber and make time. Another nice feature is an adjustable-speed motor, so you can set it at half speed or other speed choices to suit your needs. Sometimes, if you feel you are out of control, setting the dial at half or quarter speed may help you regain precision and control until you can go back to full speed with confidence.

THREAD TENSION

You should be able to adjust the upper tension and bobbin tension easily and see results. Some machines have one control that changes both the top and bottom at one time, which takes a little experimenting to find out exactly how the control works.

Even with automatic features, a sewing machine can't read your mind. It needs to be adjusted for different sewing and quilting needs. Make sure the machine you choose can be easily adjusted by you.

STITCH LENGTH

Some machines have electronic pre-determined stitch-length increments, such as 0, 0.5, 1.0, 1.5. The 0 may be too short and the 0.5 too long for those all-important securing stitches. If they are too short, an "acorn" of bobbin thread will build up on the back, or bobbin thread will appear on the top of your quilt, an unsightly problem. A dial, electronic control, or push-button control with infinite stops is best.

PRESSER-FOOT HEIGHT

For free-motion quilting, it is helpful to have a control for presser-foot pressure

(Fig. 1–2). Lessening the pressure will actually raise the presser foot a bit to allow the quilt to slide around freely while you are free-motion quilting. The foot will "skate" over the top of the quilt without getting hung up on thicker places, such as seam allowances or machine trapunto.

MOTOR

A powerful motor with variable speed settings is important. The machine will be running for long periods of time and often at a rapid rate. It needs to be able to handle this kind of use. It shouldn't get hot nor should the foot control overheat. Machines should not simply stop. If they do, something is wrong.

FREE-MOTION FEET

The darning foot is good, but there are other feet available that give more clearance and better visibility. There are metal and plastic feet for both free-motion quilting and embroidery, and it's a matter of personal preference which one you choose.

Fig. 1–2. A presser-foot pressure dial. Some machines have a lever inside the housing.

Fig. 1–3. Free-motion presser feet.

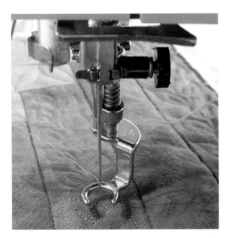

Fig. 1–4. Presser foot with shank angled to the side for greater visibility.

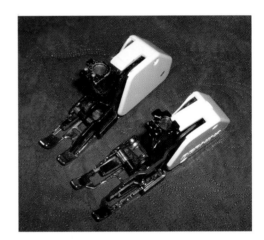

Fig. 1–5. Walking feet.

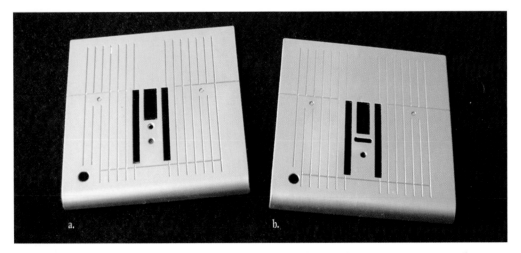

Fig. 1–6. (a) Single-hole throat plate. (b) Zigzag hole throat plate.

If you can, try them all to find which you like better (Fig. 1–3).

I like a round metal foot with the front open or cut out, or a foot large enough so the needle area is clearly visible. With the open front, you can see the line you just stitched, judge spacing accurately, avoid stitching over another line in stippling, and you can see exactly where the needle is going. Check for visibility behind the needle as well, because you will be sewing in all directions. On many of the new machines, the back of the foot is angled to the side so there is absolutely nothing in the way when you look behind the foot (Fig. 1–4).

WALKING FEET

A walking foot made for your machine is better than a generic one. The walking foot is a fantastic aid for machine quilters because it has feed dogs that complement the feed dogs in your machine (Fig.1–5). With the walking foot, all the layers are moved along at the same rate, so the top layer doesn't shift or stretch during quilting. Sometimes this foot can be as costly as four other feet, but it is worth the investment. Even on quilts for which I do nothing but quilt with a free-motion foot, I still need the walking foot to sew on the binding so it doesn't stretch the edge of the quilt.

NEEDLE-DOWN FEATURE

When the machine stops, this feature automatically lowers the needle to keep your free-motion quilting secured in place.

SINGLE-HOLE THROAT PLATE

Use this plate to replace the zigzag throat plate that comes with the machine (Fig. 1–6). The single-hole plate has a small round opening for the needle, which helps stitch quality immensely for all straight stitching, but it is especially helpful for free-motion quilting. The small hole keeps the bobbin thread in line by not allowing it to swing to the left or right as it could with the larger opening. The zigzag plate may cause poor quality stitching on curves and on side-to-side free-motion quilting.

MACHINE SERVICING

Whatever brand of machine you have now or decide to buy, be sure you have good service technicians available who will listen to you. If you do have a problem with your machine, know that they can't read your mind. Take in samples of the problem, write a simple, coherent description of the problem in case you can't talk to the technician personally, and be nice! Remember that Christmas card and bake him or her brownies. If the problem isn't fixed, take the machine back right away, don't wait for months, or complain about the service, never giving them a chance to make it right.

As a safety net, see about getting full credit for the new machine if you trade it in on a better machine within a year. Many dealers have this program, so if you find you really do want a machine with more features, or a different model, you can trade up with no financial loss.

The Sewing Area
TABLES AND CABINETS

Back when I bought my first sewing machine in the 1960s, machines came with something that is extremely important for machine quilting, a cabinet! If you wanted to take your machine to other places to sew, you bought a portable machine. So one of

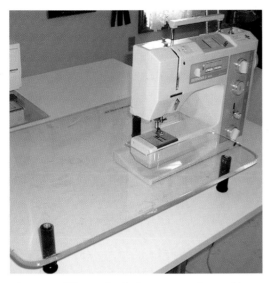

Fig. 1–7. If you don't have a sewing cabinet, an extension table can be used.

Fig. 1–8. Here's a quick and easy way to create a machine sewing table. The bottom shelf was added at just the right height.

the biggest obstacles we have to overcome now in machine quilting didn't exist then; that is, the machine now sits on top of a table, instead of down in a cabinet. With the machine so high, it is awkward to use.

In addition, most modern machines have a small free-arm. Trying to sew with only the narrow free-arm to support your quilt can be extremely frustrating and difficult. The first step is to add an extension table that fits around the free-arm and provides a larger flat area for quilting (Fig. 1–7). A flat quilting area at about 30 inches in height from the floor makes for a flat quilt. If you have to pull the part of the quilt you are working on up to the needle area and support its weight at the same time, there's a greater chance for sewing in a pleat or a pucker. Pulling at the quilt will distort it so it won't lie flat, and you can break your needle. It's also uncomfortable to quilt that way, not to mention the fatigue and pain you will experience from holding your arms up to quilt.

When I do free-motion quilting, most of the quilt rests on a large surrounding surface, so I am moving only the small portion of the quilt that is under the needle and resting my left forearm directly on the cabinet or the quilt while I work. I don't have to hold my arms up in front of me and "scrub floors!"

Before I had my current setup, I had my machine set into a small desk with the shelf the machine came with covering an opening cut out of the desk top (Fig. 1–8). I placed an old table behind the desk at the same height and a small end table to the left when I quilted. This is a simple and inexpensive arrangement, which works fine, if you have someone who can modify a desk or table for your machine.

There are inexpensive sewing tables available as well if you can't afford a cabinet. These tables are portable. Use whatever you have to create a sewing surface that will support a quilt. Even a small project needs support, and it doesn't like to be stretched and dragged up to that little platform to be quilted.

An important thing to consider is the texture of the insert that goes around the free-arm. Some of the ones I have worked with in classes are rough, like old refrigerator shelves, and moving the quilt smoothly on them is difficult. The smoother the surface, the easier it will be to machine quilt.

LIGHTING

Good lighting is important for doing the close work that machine quilting requires. A natural-spectrum light has a bulb that provides glare-free lighting which can be directed or angled onto the work area. I have a table lamp placed in *front* of my machine with the base at the right (Fig. 1–9). Just by changing the tilt of the lamp, a different lighting effect can be achieved. Placing the lamp behind the machine might work for you, but it didn't help me at all.

I sometimes turn off the light on my sewing machine and use the table lamp alone, especially when quilting on dark or hard-to-see fabrics. Any small, directional task light will work. Be wary of halogen bulbs because they can melt the front of your sewing machine if they are too close to it.

I no longer turn on my overhead room light because it seems to cast a shadow on my quilting area, which makes it more difficult to see. Using several smaller portable lamps to shine right on specific areas is a big help. If you can't see what you are quilting and are just guessing where to sew or what the stitches look like, you are fighting an uphill battle.

Machine quilting is hard on the eyes. Be sure to get regular eye exams and get the correct prescription for close vision. It made a huge difference when I had an eye exam, after many years, and got new glasses that were exactly the right prescription. I now have glasses with my reading (quilting) prescription in the entire lens instead of bifocals.

Fig. 1–9. Try putting a directional light in front of your machine.

Needles and Threads
MACHINE QUILTING NEEDLES

When I first started machine quilting, I used the recommended #80 universal needle with nylon monofilament thread and #50 three-ply cotton thread in the bobbin, and it worked well. The combination created the illusion of hand quilting. Modern electronic machines often have a mock hand-quilting programmed stitch that uses nylon thread to connect little dots of colored bobbin thread.

After making many quilts, I despaired of the large needle holes that were permanent. The bobbin thread was always visible right through the nylon thread that didn't ever fill the hole, and many times the bobbin thread popped up to the top of the quilt, which looked dreadful. Double stitching, or backtracking, over the same line of stitching caused the heavy cotton thread to build up to a thick string-like strand, and it was obvious where I had gone over a line of quilting more than once.

Now I realize that machine quilting is machine quilting, and I don't try to camouflage it or try to fool the eye into thinking it is hand quilting. Instead, I want my machine quilting to look as precise and perfect as possible, for *machine stitching*.

Recently, I have started using the smallest needle I can find for machine quilting with nylon monofilament thread. It is a #60 sharp needle, which makes a tiny, precise hole. It prevents the bobbin thread from coming through to the top or shadowing through. Along with the smaller needle, I switched to #60 two-ply cotton embroidery thread for the bobbin. If you prefer not to use nylon thread, I would also recommend this needle and the #60 cotton thread for both the top and bobbin. When double stitching is needed, the result with #60 cotton thread is a much finer line of stitches, only four-ply total, which is silky and smooth looking. Also, the new #100 or finer silk threads work well for close machine quilting.

If you are using a heavier thread, like a #40 cotton in the top and bobbin, then a larger needle will be necessary, not only to make your machine work properly, but also so you can thread the needle. For heavier threads, a #80 universal needle works well.

A #60 sharp needle is fragile, very sharp, and easily broken, not for beginners! Learn to quilt with a #70 universal needle, and when you achieve a degree of control, switch to a #70 sharp and then to the #60

sharp. You will see right away that, with no difference in your skill, your quilting looks much nicer.

If you are using heavier cotton thread for strong, utility-type quilting, a #70 sharp or jeans/denim needle works the best. They are strong, not easily broken, and make precise holes. Quilting needles are now available which are also excellent for machine quilting. I don't use them because they do not come in a small size for monofilament thread. However, their shape and strength work particularly well for piecing, and the needle sews through difficult multi-layered seam crossings very well.

Needles get dull fast during machine quilting, and when they start to sound dull or your work doesn't look as nice, change the needle. Sometimes changing the needle can make all the difference between just okay quilting and lovely quilting.

For specialty threads, like metallic or rayon, use the needle that the thread manufacturer recommends. For variegated or heavy decorative threads, use a top-stitching or embroidery needle that has a larger eye to accommodate the heavier thread. Also, consult the manufacturer's suggestions for the bobbin thread type and weight to use with these needle threads for best results, and if you don't like how the quilting is going, try something different.

Your quilt shop or sewing center can help you make a selection from the large array of needles and threads. If you buy some funky, hairy thread, don't go home and thread your machine with whatever old needle just happens to be in it. Check to make sure you get the proper needle for the thread when you buy it.

MACHINE QUILTING THREADS

During a class for machine stippling, one of my students was frustrated, angry, and near tears because her stippling wasn't looking anything at all like mine. When I sat down at her machine, the new one she was ready to throw out the window, I saw right away what the problem was. It wasn't the machine, and it wasn't her ability. It was the thread!

She had a silk-finish #40 cotton thread in the top and bobbin and had a new quilting needle, probably an #80 or larger. She was trying to use this combination to stitch shapes no bigger than a pea. I sat at her machine, checked the tension, and quilted some larger stipple shapes with lines about one-half inch apart and stitches three times longer than she was doing. The thread looked like lustrous embroidery, an embellishment for the quilt. It lay in perfect shapes, no puckering, no needle holes, lovely.

This quilter was using the wrong tools for the job she was trying to accomplish. For tiny stippling, it's best to use a small needle, fine thread, and a short stitch length. It's all a matter of proportion. She purchased the correct items and, within half an hour, was producing the kind of stippling she had wanted so much.

Look in any thread department of a quilt shop or fabric store and you will discover a huge array of threads, many marked "machine quilting thread." Which ones to try? How in the world does a beginner or even an experienced quilter know which thread will be the best? The only way to discover what will work for you for a particular project is to start testing with the basic threads and then move to some of the more unusual ones.

FEATHER SAMPLES

Cotton threads. Our quilts are usually made of cottons, so the natural choice is a 100-percent cotton thread in the top and in the bobbin. One of the best is a #50 three-ply, silk-finish cotton (Fig. 1–10, page 22). It is durable, flexible, yet beautiful and silky looking when quilted. It works well in most machines; however, it does have limitations. If you are machine quilting large shapes, simple continuous-line designs, or an all-over grid pattern, this thread is perfect. When you decide to do small stippling, double-stitched feather designs, or grids that require backtracking over the design, this thread can look too heavy.

A #40 silk-finish cotton thread is also widely used for machine quilting. It can be used in basic quilting, large meandering, and all-over straight-line grids. It looks better with a longer stitch length with more space between the quilting lines. Use it in the bobbin as well.

For heirloom-style machine quilting, #60 two-ply, silk-finish cotton embroidery thread is much nicer to use (Fig. 1–11, page 22). It has the same characteristics as #50 thread, but it is much finer. Tiny stippling, double-stitching, and feathers can be created with little obvious thread build-up. For this fine thread, a smaller needle is best, probably a #70 sharp. With this combination, there are no skipped stitches, the needle is easy to thread, and the holes are small, so the bobbin thread won't pop through to the top.

Polyester threads. Polyester thread or a cotton-covered polyester thread is much too strong and too thick for machine quilting. The thread you use should be weaker than the cotton fabric in the quilt. You should be able to break the thread by pulling on it between your two hands. If you can't break it, it is too strong and will wear and cut the quilt fabric. Lines of stitching can be easily repaired, but cut fabric is difficult to replace. The only time polyester thread should be used is when you are machine quilting with a specialty thread like a metallic, then use the polyester in the bobbin.

Machine quilting threads. There are threads labeled for machine quilting so you will think they are the only choices for the job. Most of these threads are far too heavy and stiff for the kind of quilting you see in my quilts. If they are all you have available, try them and see how they look. You may need to use a larger needle, take a longer stitch length, and avoid any of the small quilting shapes.

Silk threads. Recently, I have done some very fine machine quilting, such as closely spaced stippling and tiny feathers, with #100 silk thread, both in the needle

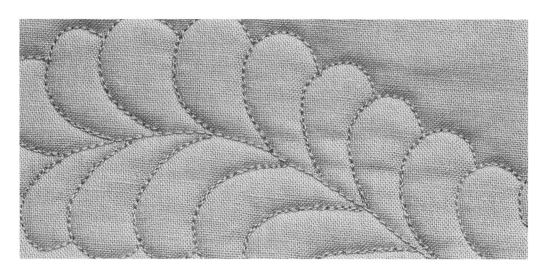

Fig. 1–10. Quilting with #50 three-ply silk-finish cotton.

Fig. 1–11. Quilting with #60 two-ply silk-finish cotton thread.

and the bobbin (Fig. 1–12). It worked wonderfully for small shapes, showed no build-up when double-stitching on feathers or grids, and my sewing machine loved it.

I used the same color in the top and bobbin to avoid tension difficulties in which one color shows as little bumps, either on the top or the back of the quilt. A neutral taupe works well on many colors, but of course, like cotton thread, you have the problem of matching or blending the colors. This is a personal choice, whether to camouflage the machine quilting stitch by matching colors or emphasize it with contrasting colors. Alternatively, you could use one neutral color throughout. The big drawback with silk thread is its expense. For a large quilt with extensive quilting, the cost would be somewhat more than for cotton thread.

Using #60 two-ply cotton embroidery thread in the bobbin with silk in the top works wonderfully too. I find that I get a nicer stitch with the cotton in the bobbin.

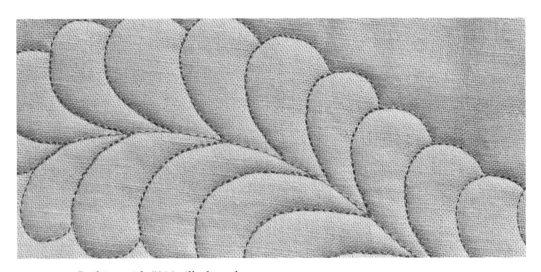

Fig. 1–12. Quilting with #100 silk thread.

Fig. 1–13. Quilting with .004 nylon monofilament thread.

Perhaps the fuzziness of the cotton helps control the thin and slippery silk thread. So I get the advantage of silk on top, with its luster and fineness for heirloom quilting, and the sturdiness of cotton on the back. It cuts the expense of using silk thread in half as well.

Monofilament threads. For years, my thread of choice has been a .004 thickness of nylon monofilament (Fig. 1–13, page 23). I have paired it with either a #50 three-ply cotton thread or recently, a #60 two-ply cotton embroidery thread in the bobbin. I have never used monofilament in the bobbin because it doesn't provide the correct strength, pliability, and tension for my stitches.

The .004 monofilament thread is very fine, and it is not like fishing line. It is soft and flexible, almost like a hair. It is easily broken when you pull it, but it will stretch and give in the finished quilt. I have never had nylon stitches break in a quilt, even with frequent usage, washing, folding, and making the bed. This thread has come to have a bad reputation because of incorrect usage. If the stitches are big, you will definitely see that it is nylon and notice its sheen. However, if the stitch length is quite short, it looks indistinguishable from silky cotton thread. Using smoke-colored or lightly tinted nylon monofilament thread cuts down its visibility and sheen on medium- to dark-colored fabrics.

As for durability, there have been so many questions about how long monofilament will last, and the answer is, "I don't know!" Some say it will fall apart and disintegrate in 60 years. We haven't had it for that long, so we cannot predict what will happen. Based on common sense and observation of textile durability, I can only guess. When we moved into our first home, we had a commercially hemmed, store-bought curtain in the sunny south window of our main bathroom. It was subjected to heat, UV rays, and humidity. The curtain fabric was a cotton print, which was hemmed with quite heavy nylon invisible thread. The fabric faded and disintegrated in spots, but the hem stayed firm and fine, the thread as tough as ever.

Silks and cottons and all natural-fiber textiles are fragile and must be protected from heat, humidity, and UV rays. Even then, they will deteriorate with time and use. As for nylon, I would use every safeguard to ensure its long life, the same as with cotton thread. My oldest quilts made with nylon thread are about 12 years old, and I have had no problems with breakage, weakening, or disintegration, even with much use and washing. The jury is still out on this question. If you feel this thread is not for you and you don't want to chance it, then it would be best to choose something else.

One of the most frequent questions I am asked is why I use nylon monofilament thread. There are many reasons, but basically I use it because it eliminates the problem of color matching, it doesn't cover my quilt top with heavy machine stitching, it allows me to quilt exceptionally fine designs and closely spaced stippling, it permits me to double stitch over a line of stitching several times with no visible build-up, and it doesn't make my quilt look "thready."

Machine Quilting Needles and Threads

NEEDLE	CHARACTERISTICS	THREADS
#80 Universal	Good all-around choice for piecing, quilting. Has rounded end, makes fairly large hole in quilt.	#40 cotton, #50 cotton, #60 cotton, rayons, many specialty threads
#70 Universal	Rounded end, leaves a smaller hole in quilt than the #80, so not as many problems with bobbin pop-ups.	#50 cotton, #60 cotton, nylon monofilament, invisible polyester, water soluble
#60 Universal	Rounded end, leaves small hole.	#60 cotton or finer thread like invisible polyester, #100 silk, nylon monofilament, water soluble
#70 Jeans/denim	Pointed, sharp end, leaves smaller cleaner hole in quilt, strong and stable needle even for beginners.	#50 cotton, #60 cotton, nylon monofilament, invisible polyester, #100 silk, water soluble
#70 Sharp	Very sharp, good for more fragile fabrics like synthetics and silk, leaves small hole in quilt.	#50 cotton, #60 cotton, nylon monofilament, invisible polyester, #100 silk, water soluble
#60 Sharp	Finest needle for very close machine quilting through cotton batt; leaves tiny hole, can't see through the hole easily to bobbin thread; prevents bobbin pop-ups; fragile and easy to break; good for silks and fine fabrics.	#60 cotton, nylon monofilament, invisible polyester, #100 silk, water soluble
#75 Quilting	Sharp point for clean small hole, strong, good for beginners and for opaque thicker threads like #50 cotton or rayons, very good for piecing through many seam allowances.	#50 cotton, #60 cotton, rayon, silk, water soluble, specialty threads like variegated
Embroidery, top stitching, Metafil	Used for special purposes and threads, has coated eye or larger eye to prevent fraying of threads.	specialty threads like metallic and embroidery

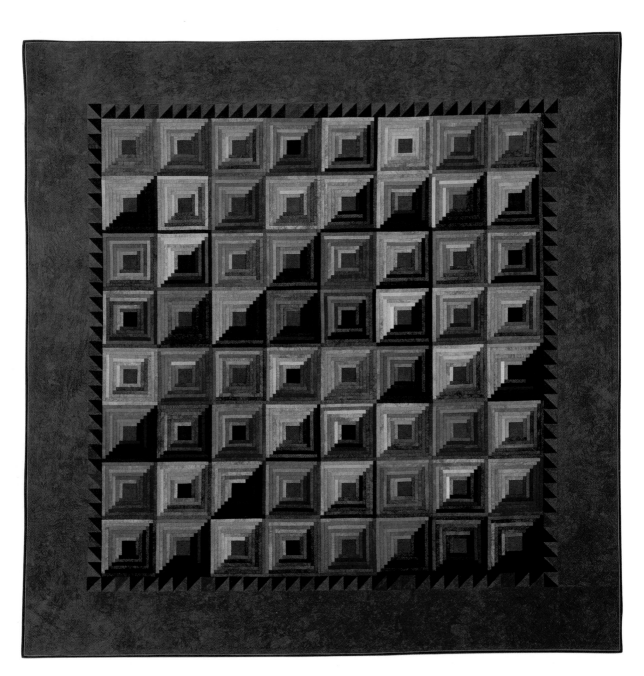

THROUGH A GLASS DARKLY: AN AMERICAN MEMORY, 80" x 80". These Log Cabin blocks contain hand-dyed cottons. The piece is machine quilted with nylon monofilament and silk threads. Gradations of color are based on my cat Fluffy's fur. (2001 Pfaff Master Award for Machine Artistry at the International Quilt Association Quilt Show; First Place AQS Show 2002; Best of Show and judged "Masterpiece Quilt" by NQA, 2002.)

FABRIC PREPARATION

When I was showing my quilt OCTOBER MORNING, which has deep reds and a lighter lilac background, I was asked if I have had problems with red fabrics bleeding. I answered quickly and truthfully, "Not when I get done with them!" I use a pre-washing system that prevents bleeding problems with dark-colored fabrics.

Whether or not to pre-wash is a personal choice. One of my first experiences in quilting was making a red and white Kansas Troubles quilt. It had many tiny triangles throughout, all cut from different red fabrics. Well, of course, I pre-washed the reds separately, then dumped them all together in the washer with cold water and some quilt soap. After the quilt was finished, I washed it in cool water and more quilt soap, only to find that one of those reds had bled horribly into the surrounding white background fabric. The rest of the reds were fine, but it only takes one bleeder to teach a lesson.

From that quilt on, I have always pre-washed my fabrics in hot water, one at a time, until no color is left in the rinse water, and then washed them all one more time in the washing machine. I've never had another problem with fabrics bleeding.

Machine piecing and quilting are dependent on how the fabric is prepared. Many quilters use fabric fresh from the bolt, but I like to prepare mine for piecing and quilting so that I know how it will react when subjected to all the things that will happen to it.

Pre-washing Method

DIVIDE FABRICS INTO STACKS

Sort fabrics according to value: lights, mediums, darks, and maybe even a special pile of fabrics you have a hunch will bleed. Usually the lights and mediums can be put right into the washer without any testing.

For light fabrics, I use very hot water and a little quilt soap dissolved in a jar of water. Add to the wash about one cup of white vinegar to help eliminate possible allergens, such as mold, mildew, and dust mites. A delicate or hand-wash cycle is best because it won't tangle the cloth as badly as a normal cycle. A small amount of liquid fabric softener can be added to the final rinse to help control wrinkling. After the wash cycle, dry the fabrics on medium heat with a cool-down cycle, so that, when taken from the dryer immediately and folded for storage, they are smooth and easy to work with.

TEST DARK FABRICS INDIVIDUALLY

Dark fabrics, such as reds, purples, and greens, can be treated exactly the same way, only be sure to immerse each one in a white sink or bowl with hot water and a bit of quilt soap. Most of them will lose a little dye or no dye and can go right into the washer with the rest of the fabrics. However, some will need repeated soakings in this hot water bath until most of the excess dye has been removed. If you should have a fabric that keeps on bleeding after several washings, common sense says not to use it.

Hand-dyed fabrics are particularly prone to releasing a lot of excess dye. Sometimes the rinse water looks like grape juice or dark coffee. Keep rinsing until the water is clear. Then all the dark fabrics can be washed together in the washer the same way as for the lights and mediums.

Starch – the Right Stuff

When working with members of the "no-ironing" generation, raised on perma-press and knits, I have to carefully explain the benefits of using starch when pressing fabrics for quilts and during the entire construction of a quilt. It stabilizes the fabric, gives it a "hand" similar to that of crisp new fabric, and keeps pieces from becoming distorted or stretched under the presser foot.

If used heavily, starch also makes a good stabilizer for background fabric in appliqué. Commercial starches are available in liquid and aerosol form, as well as powdered for mixing your own. Because of my sensitivity toward chemicals and scents, I had to devise my own recipe from basic household cornstarch, used to thicken sauces. It is an estimated recipe, like most of my cooking, and if you don't like the consistency, thin it by diluting it or make it thicker by adding more starch at the beginning.

Spray Starch Recipe

Dissolve one-half teaspoon of cornstarch with a few tablespoons of cold water in a two-cup, heat-proof glass measuring cup. Boil about one cup of water, add it to this mixture, and stir constantly. The mixture will turn from chalky white to milky translucent. Add cool water to make two cups of solution. Let it cool to room temperature and then pour it into a pump spray bottle. Shake it well before spritzing the fabric. There are no preservatives, so you will need to make a fresh batch every week.

STARCHING TIPS

• **Wash and dry your fabrics,** but do not starch and press them until ready to use.

• **Lightly press the fabrics first,** then spray with starch and press again. Be careful not to move the iron too much so you don't stretch or distort the damp fabrics.

• **If you get a build-up** of white flaky stuff on your fabric, thin the starch with more water. Every so often, use a damp terry-cloth rag to wipe off the iron when it is cool. White vinegar can be used to dissolve any starch buildup. Be sure to use the vinegar on a cool iron, because the vinegar will steam on a hot iron. If this happens, it's a good way to unclog congested sinuses, but your house will smell like pickles.

• **Protect your ironing board** with a length of plain muslin. About two yards of muslin is a good length. Lay one end on the ironing board and, as it gets stiff with starch and threads, pull a new section of muslin onto the ironing board (Fig. 1–14). Keep moving the muslin along until the entire length has been used. Then wash it with hot water and soap, dry and re-use.

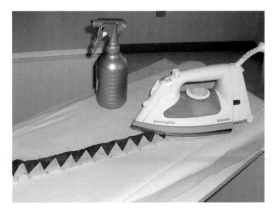

Fig. 1–14. Use a couple of yards of muslin to protect your ironing board from starch.

• **If you get scorch marks**, your iron is too hot, or you are holding it on the fabric too long.

• **Apply starch to the right side** of the fabric, which is pressed from this side as well. If you don't plan to wash the finished quilt, use commercial sizing products instead. They provide crispness without the hazy look that regular starch can produce.

• **Press and starch the backing** for a quilt. I use a shorter stitch length and press seam allowances open on backings. After quilting, the seams are almost invisible. The starch gives the backing stability for machine quilting, and it really reduces the occurrence of pleats or puckers. It also makes the quilt glide over the machine bed easily, almost like it has silicone on the back. Starch makes for much easier handling of the entire quilt.

• **If you run out of starch** during a project, use plain water. It will activate the starch already in the fabric and work much the same as an additional application of the starch mixture.

• **Don't starch your fabrics for storage.** Starch will attract critters like silverfish. Wash and fold your fabrics, then when you are ready to cut, go ahead and press them with starch.

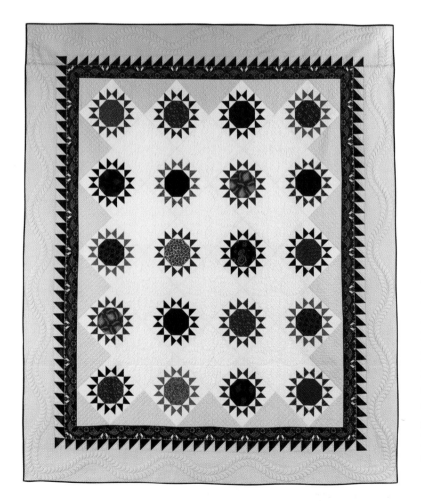

ARNIE'S RISING STARS, 85" x 98". This octagon star pattern contains colors inspired by my orange and white cat Arnie. (Mountain Mist® cotton batt, original trapunto feather designs, quilted with nylon monofilament thread. Second place award at the 1996 AQS Quilt Show and Contest, and Wisconsin winner in Land's End Good Housekeeping "All American Quilt Contest," 1996.)

BATTING CHOICE

Growing up with my grandmother's scrap quilts made me want quilts just like her wonderful flat, puckered, soft cotton quilts, but everything I tried gave me a modern, puffy look. Then I discovered cotton batts for machine quilting. Cotton batting is so thin that the entire quilt can be rolled to fit in the machine and quilted with a walking or darning foot.

TOP: **Grandmother's quilt.** BOTTOM: **Close-up of block.**

Cotton Batting

Cotton batting is the heart and soul of my system of machine quilting. Not only does a thin cotton batt allow the quilt to fit in the machine, but the batt shrinks when washed to give the quilt a nice old-fashioned, puckered look. Cotton is soft, flat, and flexible, nothing at all like the polyester I used at first. Plus, a quilt made with cotton batting is wonderful to sleep under because it is a natural fiber which breathes. Also, the surface texture of a cotton batt helps to keep the quilt layers from shifting during quilting. Using polyester is much

like quilting a greased marshmallow, which is slippery and puffy.

Today there are many kinds of cotton batts for you to choose from, and they all have different properties. It's a good idea to experiment to find out what effect you want and which batt will produce it.

MODERN LOOK

If you want a look that is smooth and thin, choose a cotton batt that you can pre-wash and one that has the thickness you desire. If you pre-wash it before layering it in your quilt, you won't get that puckered look, and the quilt will stay flat and smooth (see photo below, left). There are many batts available now, and they come in different weights. Some batts have a scrim (woven layer). Some are made from cotton lint held together with a coating of sizing. The lint type cannot be pre-washed. Check the package instructions to see what the manufacturer suggests in regard to pre-washing and care.

ANTIQUE LOOK

For an antique look, choose a batt that has a high amount of shrinkage (five percent) and needs close quilting, then do not pre-wash it. Layer the quilt with this batt right from the package and wash the quilt when it is finished. Mountain Mist® 100-percent cotton and Fairfield's Cotton Classic® are two old-fashioned batts that will produce this look. Be sure you quilt closely enough so the batting won't shift and bunch (see photo below, right).

If the quilt is air dried, it will shrink and pucker nicely, but if more shrinkage or a softer quilt is desired, the quilt can be dried in the dryer set on low. Plan ahead for the shrinkage when you are determining the size of a finished quilt. With a Cotton Classic batt and pre-washed cotton fabrics, a 95-inch square quilt, when washed in lukewarm water and dried flat on the floor, will shrink down to about 90 inches. Drying it in the dryer will cause even more shrinkage.

Quilt by Erma Hinterberg with pre-washed cotton batt.

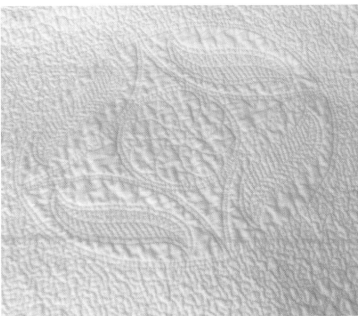

Quilt with cotton batt, not pre-washed.

Make various samples from different batts and wash and dry them to determine the look you like before you commit to using a batt in a large project. Some batting companies offer small sample squares of various batts, which you can try and compare.

Shrinkage not only gives the look of a hand-quilted quilt, but it forgives such mistakes as uneven stitches. A beginner's quilting will be camouflaged when the quilt is washed, blocked, and dried. You would have to look carefully at the line of stitching to see whether it is even or not. The combination of shrinkage and the use of nylon monofilament thread can give the illusion of hand quilting and will also camouflage a beginner's mistakes.

Cotton or washable wool batting is like our hair. It is a natural fiber that will take on the shape you choose when it is wet and will dry to that shape. If you can remember setting your hair in pin curls with bobbie pins, then you can imagine how pliable a wet cotton-batt quilt is. After you are done quilting and have bound the quilt, wash and rinse it thoroughly. Straighten it, making sure the corners are square, then lay the wet quilt flat for drying and stretch those borders flat.

Cats love quilts – Arnie and his blue ribbon quilt.

When the quilt is dry, it will be the way you positioned it when wet. If it is not to your liking, re-wet and re-block it.

Comparing Brands

The following list describes some of the batts I use and recommend:

MOUNTAIN MIST

The 100% cotton and Blue Ribbon® cotton are easy to quilt, give a flat appearance, do not become distorted when hung, and shrink when washed to give an antique, puckered look. They are easy to use because the layers do not shift while being quilted. Read the package directions for specific information, like distance between quilting lines and shrinkage. Blue Ribbon can be quilted up to two inches apart. Do not pre-wash these batts!

FAIRFIELD

Cotton Classic® is made of 80-percent cotton and 20-percent polyester. It is easy to use and has been improved to be softer and thicker. It is still thin and flat and has a nice texture, so the quilt layers stay in place during quilting. It also creates a lovely antique appearance and can be quilted up to three inches apart. It is stiffer than Hobbs' Heirloom and some of the newer batts.

Soft Touch® cotton is 100-percent cotton. It has no scrim, so it is soft, thin, and cottony, like a piece of baby flannel. You can use it for hand quilting because it has that cottony look, yet it is still easy to needle.

HOBBS

Heirloom® Cotton is 80-percent cotton, 20-percent polyester. It will shrink slightly. This is the best batt for beginners, and the directions for use are complete on the package. It has great loft (puffiness), and it doesn't need a lot of background quilting. It is manufactured to be like a blanket, so it is easy to handle. It's a little thicker than the previously described batts, but it will still shrink and give dimension to your quilting.

Organic Heirloom® is an extremely nice, soft, all-cotton batt that will help your quilt remain soft even if closely quilted.

QUILTER'S DREAM

Quilter's Dream®, an all-cotton batt, is like a blanket. It comes in several weights, but I have used and loved the thinnest option. It is good for both hand and machine quilting. The deluxe version I tried was so thick and heavy, it was difficult to work with, but it was really dense if that's what you want. The thinner versions are easier to use for machine quilting, and they are nice for clothing because there is minimal shrinkage. They stay relatively soft even after heavy machine quilting.

Wool Batting

Some "new-generation" washable wool batts work wonderfully for machine quilting. They have a higher loft than cotton batts, and they are lighter and fluffier. They do not get as stiff when heavily quilted, and the designs do not need the addition of trapunto for definition. Washing a quilt with one of the new wool batts does provide some shrinkage, but the quilting designs will not get lost in the puckering.

Hobbs' Heirloom Wool® is a lovely batt, which can be washed in cool water and air dried. The loft and lightness will come right back. There is some shrinkage. It is easy to needle for hand quilting, and it is soft and warm. It can be quilted three inches apart. It is especially nice for close stippling because it does not get stiff.

BACKING FABRIC

One of my students reported a problem with a backing fabric that drove her to despair as she tried to free-motion quilt. Unfortunately, the white fabric she had chosen for the backing was an all-over small print, a "white-on-white." However, the small print contained something in it similar to latex that actually caused the fabric to stick to the surface of her sewing area. It would not budge. It seemed like the fabric had grippers attached to it to prevent it from moving smoothly, so her stitches were uneven and difficult to control. Her muscles ached. Her frustration was intense, but she finished it and reported to me that she'd never choose that type of backing again.

This student's experience points out the importance of backing fabric to successful quilting. There are some things you need to know when choosing a backing. Color, consistency, and print scale make a vital difference. Don't buy sale fabric or fabric that you don't like and think to yourself, "I can always use it as a backing," because the backing selection can make or break your machine quilting.

Choose the Right Color

No matter what your thread choices are, the color of the backing is a crucial ingredient for good-looking machine quilting. If you are using invisible nylon thread, the choice is doubly important because the bobbin thread may show on the front of the quilt. It can pop up to the front because of the tight tension of the nylon thread. It will also show if your needle hole is too large, for example, if you use a #80 universal needle.

A good rule of thumb to follow is to choose the color of the backing so it is no darker than the lightest color on the front of the quilt, especially if you have a light background. Consequently, your matching bobbin thread will blend in with the lightest color on the top and not be noticeable. If it should show on a darker fabric, it can be colored in with a pen. I use a very fine point .1 permanent-ink pen, used for writing on quilts, to place a dot of color on the light thread (Fig. 1–15). The pen doesn't need to match the fabric color exactly. A dark brown can be used with many dark colors.

If you use an opaque thread, such as rayon, cotton, or silk in both the top and the bobbin, it is best to use the same color in both, even if the thread types are different. For example, using a red rayon on top and a #60 matching red cotton in the bobbin would work well, and you wouldn't see any tension irregularities.

Start by deciding what color of thread you will use in the top of the quilt for the areas with the most quilting, then pick the same color for the bobbin thread. Choose a backing fabric that will blend in with or camouflage this bobbin thread.

Many problems can be eliminated by a little careful planning in what color of backing you use. I once made the mistake of using a neutral tan on the back of a quilt I had quilted in red silk thread. It was a constant struggle to keep the bits of tan bobbin thread from showing on the red, or the red thread from showing on the back. I should have used a red print backing and red bobbin thread, then it would have been perfect, painless, and faster. Red bobbin thread on the tan backing would have been fine as another option.

Choose the Right Fabric

For machine quilting, knowing the properties of various backing fabrics will help you decide which ones will work the best for you. As mentioned, some white-on-white prints don't work well for machine quilting because they don't allow the quilt to move smoothly in the machine. Some colored prints have this same problem. Parts of the print seem to be "sticky", because they have an extra-thick coating of dye or rubbery pigment. If you plan on quilting entirely with

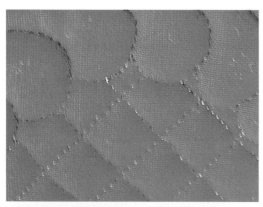
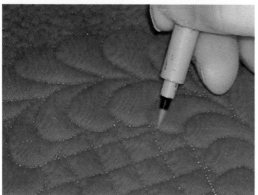

Fig. 1–15. (a) Bobbin thread pop-ups. (b) Inking pop-ups.

feed dogs and a walking foot, then this problem would be minimized.

Use 100-percent cotton fabrics and give the backing a trial run before buying 10 yards. Buy only a quarter or half yard first and see if it works with your quilt top's background fabric, thread, and batting choices.

PRINT OR PLAIN?

If you are a beginner and want to camouflage your stitches on the back, pick a busy print, such as a floral or a large-scale print, so that the stitches don't show and any unevenness is hidden (Fig. 1–16).

Avoid geometric prints. It is all but impossible to align straight quilting lines with the printed lines in a fabric.

THREAD COUNT

A fabric with a looser weave or a lower thread count seems to accommodate all the things we ask of a backing fabric. The more densely woven fabrics tend to pleat and pucker much more easily. A fabric whose grain and consistency look about the same as a good quality muslin works well. Plan to experiment with different fabrics, and when you find one line or one brand that you like, use it over and over in different colors and patterns.

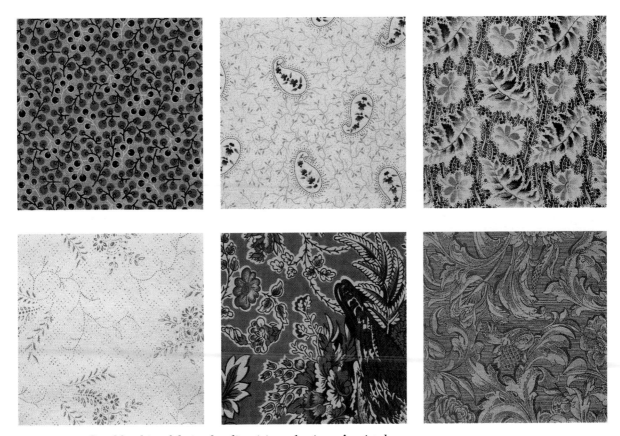

Fig. 1–16. Good backing fabrics for disguising a beginner's mistakes.

BACKING SIZE

The edges of a quilt are the most difficult to machine quilt. It would seem that they would be the easiest because they are less bulky, but because there is nothing on the right side of the quilt to hang on to, it is hard to stabilize the outside edge and keep it in control.

One thing that helps is to cut the backing fabric about three or four inches larger than the quilt top all around. When the quilt is layered, this extra backing is folded over the raw edges and pinned down to the top through all the layers. The fold keeps the edges clean and neat and keeps the pieced seams at the edges from coming out and fraying. The folded edge also makes a nice handle to grip when quilting at the edge (Fig. 1–17).

Trim the edges of the backing fabric with a rotary cutter so the cut edge doesn't fray easily. Those frayed threads can float under the quilt during quilting and get quilted in, causing time-consuming removal with tweezers later.

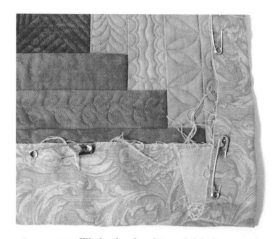

Fig. 1–17. With the backing folded over the edge of the quilt, you have something to grip while quilting.

EXTRA-WIDE FABRIC

We now have available many options in extra-wide backing fabrics, usually over 100 inches wide. These can be used for machine quilting, even though when I first considered them, I worried that the extra width, with no stabilizing seam down the center, might cause them to sag, much like an over-used mattress. Not so, they work great. I have found some to be too stiff, however, and even after washing and drying, they are still too stiff.

GRAIN LINE

One of the most important considerations when buying yardage for a quilt back is its grain line (Fig. 1–18). Fabric is most stable along the lengthwise grain, which

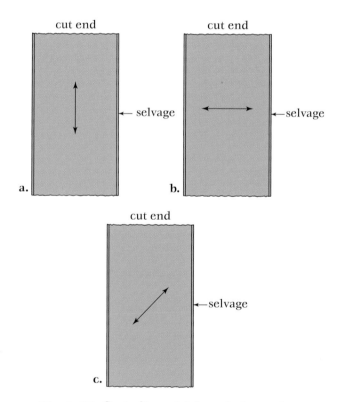

Fig. 1–18. Grain lines. (a) Lengthwise grain, (b) crosswise grain, (c) bias grain.

runs parallel to the selvages. It is less stable along the crosswise grain, which goes from selvage to selvage. Fabric stretches the most on the bias.

It is important to position the backing so the lengthwise grain runs from top to bottom, even if the quilt is square. This placement of the grain line will give the quilt stability during machine quilting and when it is hanging on a wall. If you first quilt any stabilizing lines, they need to be sewn from top to bottom also. The stabilizing lines must run in the same direction as the backing grain line to prevent pleats, puckers, and distortion.

Piecing the Backing

If your quilt is wider than the average useable fabric width of about 40 inches, it will be necessary to trim the selvages off of two or more fabric panels and sew them together lengthwise. I never worry about where the seams will end up on the back of a quilt.

Use a shorter stitch length, #60 two-ply cotton thread, and a #70 sharp needle when piecing a backing. Press the seam allowances open to make them flat. Make sure your tension is correct so the seams don't pucker.

Starch the backing

One of the most important things in preparing a quilt backing is to give it a final pressing with starch, on the right side of the fabric. Starch gives the backing stability so it won't stretch, pleat, and pucker, and it makes the backing glass-smooth so it slides over the sewing surface easily.

MARKING

The question comes up over and over again, "What do you mark your quilt with?" For machine quilting, it's necessary to have a marking tool that goes on readily; can be seen easily during quilting, especially backward; and comes off completely, even when it is under dense sewing-machine stitching. I don't use pencils because it's difficult to erase pencil lines under machine quilting. They are there for eternity! I use two markers, the blue water-soluble pen and the white water-soluble pencil.

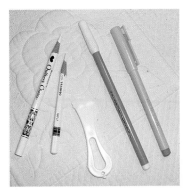

BLUE WASH-OUT MARKERS

The most maligned, yet most useful tool we machine quilters use, is probably the blue water-soluble pen, also called a blue wash-out marker. I can't tell you how many times I have been answering questions at a show, only to see jaws drop and eyes widen in horror when I explain that I do, indeed, mark the entire quilt top with a blue wash-out marker.

The one thing to remember is to submerge the finished quilt in cool water to remove the markings completely. Next, a gentle washing with quilt soap and warm water helps remove any residue. A light misting of water is not enough. With that in mind, let's find out what makes this marker so popular.

This marker is like a felt-tip pen, and the ink is bright turquoise blue. It leaves a smooth bright line that is visible on many fabric prints and colors, which makes it ideal for the machine quilter because the line being followed is very obvious. No light pencil sketching here! You need a mark that is easy to see and easy to remove after it's quilted.

The marker's best attributes are its transparency and brightness, and the stitches can be seen through the ink color. This feature is invaluable when backtracking (double stitching), as for feathers, grids, or other traditional designs that are not continuous lines. The blue marks are much better than white chalky marks or dark pen lines, which really obscure the stitching. Then, it's just a guess to try to hit the line right a second time. The bad reputation of the blue marker has largely been the result of incorrect usage.

HERE ARE SOME TIPS TO HELP YOU USE THIS TOOL EFFECTIVELY:

• **Don't let it sit.** Don't mark something with this pen and leave it sit for years, waiting to be quilted. Mark and quilt it right away. Over time, the marks may lighten considerably or even disappear because of the humidity in the air.

• **Avoid heat and light.** After the quilt has been marked, don't subject it to heat or light. No packing it in a hot car to take to a workshop. No letting it sit on a table with the sun beating in on it. No pressing it with an iron or placing it on a hot TV.

• **Don't press hard.** You will flatten the tip and make the line way too dark and wide for good quilting. Also, the pen won't fit in a stencil if the end is all smashed out of shape. And, finally, pressing hard will move the quilt fabric around so your design will be inaccurate.

• **Protect markers.** A fine-line marker dries out fast and should be kept for use in precise marking tasks, like straight lines or grids. The more accurately these lines are drawn, the more precisely they can be quilted. Remember to replace the cap after each use.

• **Use several markers.** For a large quilt top, I use three or four markers and rotate them after five minutes or so. I store them flat in a zippered plastic bag, not upright in a mug. If they get frequent rest periods, they re-charge faster and last much longer.

• **Date your markers.** Place a piece of tape on each marker, with the purchase date written on it. I can't tell you how many times I have opened a new marker and put it down, then couldn't tell which was the new one. Masking tape with the date written on it works great and will help you rotate your stock, just like in a grocery store.

• **Starch the quilt top.** Starch helps to keep the marking chemical from penetrating the quilt. The ink will also go on more easily and last longer.

• **Check marks as you go.** When you are using a light table to trace a design, it is difficult to see if the blue marker is leaving enough of a line and if all the lines have been traced. Periodically, turn off the light under the tracing table and check to see that the lines are visible. I have traced an entire border design on a small quilt only to find that the marker had run dry.

• **Use blue markers on dark fabric.** A blue marker shows up fine, even on dark fabrics. I have used it on a dark cocoa-brown solid, and it could be seen clearly. It was even more visible in the sewing machine with the light on it.

• **Try different brands.** Some pens have hard scratchy tips; some are soft. Experiment to see what works best.

• **Fixing mistakes.** If you make a mistake when marking, either draw some x's through the line or use a cotton swab dipped in cool water to erase the line. The down side of this method is having to wait for the fabric to dry, usually 10 to 20 minutes. Time for a break!

• **Test your markers.** Remember to always test markers on your fabrics. Sometimes, the chemicals in one fabric's dye will react to a marker, which may cause problems.

Will the markers damage quilts? We don't really know, but completely soaking and washing the quilt after it is finished will help prevent any problems. It also helps to quilt as soon after marking as possible, so the ink is on the quilt for only a short time. Personally, I have had only excellent results with this product, and I believe it is a great aid for machine-quilted designs.

WHITE WASH-OUT PENCILS

As with the blue markers, there are several brands of white water-soluble pencils. They are not made of chalk. White wash-out pencils are constructed like regular lead pencils and can be sharpened in a pencil sharpener. Use them just like a pencil, and if you press down firmly but lightly, they will not break and will provide you with a clear, white line on dark fabrics.

They do pull or drag on fabric and are more difficult to work with than the blue pens. If you place a piece of flannel, a rotary cutting mat, or something underneath the quilt to cushion it a bit, the pencil will work better. Because batting is so soft, it is difficult to use these pencils over batting. Therefore, it's best to mark before layering.

These white pencils go on easily, and the marks will last through the entire quilting process, unlike other marking tools, such as chalk. That is why they are especially good for machine quilting, and the marks will stand up to all the handling.

REMOVING MARKINGS

I try to quilt to one side of the marked quilting lines, which leaves the line exposed and much easier to remove. To remove the markings, spray with water. Really saturate the quilt and let it sit for a minute or so to dissolve the marks. Sometimes, they won't disappear with just water. It may take some elbow grease as well. I use a soft children's toothbrush to go over the markings lightly, while still wet, and brush them away. They usually come out easily and quickly. Don't brush or scrub too hard because you will damage the fabric and remove the dye.

If plain water and a toothbrush don't remove the marks completely, you may have to get out the big guns and make up a solution that will safely dissolve the marks. I use a combination of water, rubbing alcohol, and a drop of liquid detergent. (Use Joy or Palmolive because some detergents can set the markings.) Dip the toothbrush in this mixture and lightly brush the marks until they are gone. Finally, a gentle wash in the washer with some quilt soap and warm water will remove the cleaning solution and any marker residue.

Sometimes marks look like they have been completely removed only to reappear when the quilt has dried or when it is under a fluorescent light, which really shows up traces of white. If possible, use one of these lights or a full-spectrum daylight lamp to clearly illuminate the quilt so you can see if there are any remaining marks.

Fig. 1–19. Pin basting a Log Cabin quilt.

PIN BASTING

Holding the three layers of a quilt together for machine quilting is done primarily by basting with safety pins. My first quilt was basted with every safety pin I could find in the house, and then I tried straight pins when I ran out. I found out very fast that a rolled up quilt becomes a dangerous porcupine with those straight pins sticking out all over.

How many pins? My general rule of thumb is to pin every four to five inches and more closely when necessary to keep the design in place or to keep tricky areas from shifting (Fig. 1–19). Any closer than that makes it too difficult to quilt around the pins and adds too much weight to the quilt. In a bed-sized quilt, I use hundreds of pins, which weigh a lot. I take them out as I quilt to reduce the weight and get them out of my way.

Even if they are not needed any longer, leave in a few pins here and there to act as handles to help you grip the quilt for free-motion quilting.

What size and type? The basic #2 safety pin is all-purpose and works well. I like to use the smaller #1 pins around the quilting designs because I know my free-motion foot will clear them more easily. The holes they leave in the quilt go away after the quilt is washed or wetted. The new bent pins are nice, but I prefer the regular straight ones.

Where do you begin? I begin in the center and work out toward the edges, completely pinning the area on the table.

After that area has been pinned, I release the clips or tape holding the backing taut, move the quilt so an unpinned area is on the table, re-clip the backing, and pin the new area.

Where do you place pins? Plan ahead for pin placement. It is much easier to place the pins in positions that will allow the machine to move freely than to continually move them when they get in the way. It makes for fewer pleats and less distortion if the quilt is done with minimal moving of pins.

I also check to see how close my machine's foot, either walking or free-motion, needs to be to the pins for adequate clearance to determine where to put the pins. With experience, you will be able to look at a seam and know exactly how far away from it the pin needs to be.

A simple thing to remember is pin where you are not going to quilt. Pin parallel to the vertical seam lines, spacing the pins between the lines. Keep the pins straight and parallel to the seams so they won't catch on the presser foot during quilting. If the pins cross some of the horizontal seams, it won't matter because, when those seams are stitched, the pins will have been removed.

Can you move a pin? Yes, you can move pins, and it is a good idea to do so if it looks like they will be in the way or if they are distorting the quilt top as you quilt. One of the biggest advantages to using safety pins is they can be moved if necessary.

What about thread basting? Thread basting does not work well for machine quilting. It does not allow for changes during quilting, and it catches on the presser foot. Also, the thread is difficult to remove after it has been stitched under lines of machine quilting. Save thread basting for hand-quilting projects.

When do you remove pins? I remove the safety pins as I quilt, after they are no longer needed. I also remove them directly before I reach an area if they will interfere with my free-motion quilting or catch on the foot. By the time you do the background quilting, most of the pins will have been removed, and it will be much easier to handle the quilt without them.

If you make a mistake and have the layers positioned incorrectly or decide to change something and need to take out the pins and start over, wait a day or two so the stress on your hands and lower back won't be as great. Have a friend over to help, play some music, gossip, and have fun.

What do you do with the edges? When all the sides and corners, as well as the center, have been pinned and the quilt is pinned right out to the very edge, remove the clips and release the tension on the backing. Fold the extra batting and backing over the edges of the quilt. Pin the backing to the edge of the quilt, folding in the corners and pinning them as well. Covering the raw edges like this will protect them while the quilt is being handled and will keep the batting from shedding all over the quilt. It also keeps curious cats from eating the exposed cotton batting, something my Hillary can tell you is her favorite snack.

Quilting Technique

Equipment and supplies comprise the hardware you will need for machine quilting, but there are also techniques to be learned that will allow you to use these things to best advantage.

Get a Grip!

While watching beginning quilters poke and prod, push, and pull their quilting samples, I realized how important the way you hold a quilt can be. The most common syndrome is what I call "scrubbing floors," in which the quilter pushes down hard on the quilt with palms flat, using the quilt to scrub down the the sewing table. Face intent, muscles tensed, breathing minimally, the student will try so hard to move that quilt back and forth, with her elbows in the air and her shoulders hunched up to her ears. If you recognize yourself in this description, you are not alone. Most of the problems with fatigue and poor stitch quality do not come from a bad sewing machine, but from pilot error.

There are several ways to hold a quilt, and sometimes the situation will call for one way, and sometimes it is necessary to try a different grip to get the amount of control you need for the area you are quilting.

PRESSING HANDS FLAT

I find it difficult to control the stitch length if I press down on the quilt with my palms flat on the quilt (Fig. 1–20). The quilt seems to jerk unevenly when I use this method. However, sometimes it is necessary to really flatten an area and hold it taut, especially areas near the edge of the quilt. When I quilt a feather design, I quilt the central line, or "spine," first and use this flat grip to hold the entire area of the design firm and flat. Then, when I quilt the feathers themselves, I use the next method, hands as a "hoop."

HANDS AS A HOOP

For my favorite grip, I use my right hand to grab onto the quilt roll, using it as a handle, and extend my right index finger and thumb to form the right side of a "hoop." With my left hand, I scrunch up a section of the quilt, and use my left index finger and thumb to form the opposite side of the hoop (Fig. 1–21). By holding the quilt taut and at the same time lifting it slightly, I can get nice control and even stitches. The downside of this method is the considerable stress it places on the hand and its tendons, nerves, and muscles, so I vary my methods to relieve stress and take plenty of breaks to relieve the tension on my hands.

QUILTING AIDS

Some quilters find the following aids helpful: rubber finger tips, latex surgical gloves, cotton gloves with sticky dots on the palm, hoops made for machine quilting, and pads that grip the quilt (Fig. 1–22). For me, less is more, and I don't like the cumbersome feel of these things between me and the quilt, reducing my sense of touch and control. However, I have seen some beginners founder helplessly in trying to control the quilt and get even stitches, then they improve dramatically with one of these machine quilting aids. Try them out and see if they work for you.

One of the simplest aids is a piece of rubbery, open-weave shelf liner that prevents dishes from sliding around. Because it is thin and flexible, it can be cut into pieces about the size of index cards and placed between your hands and the quilt to provide extra traction and control.

The only thing I use is Neutrogena® Norwegian Formula hand cream for extra-dry skin. It is non-greasy but makes my hands sticky. The cream provides just enough extra traction control for me to successfully handle the quilt. I keep some at my machine at all times and use a dab every time I begin to quilt. Don't try to type after using it though. The keys will stick to your fingers.

Sometimes it's the little things in machine quilting that make so much difference. In this case, it was using hand cream to improve my grip. A new needle or a smaller needle, different thread, a single-hole throat plate, a cone thread holder, a new light, these are the small things that provide big results.

So, where are your arms?

All this talk of hands, fingers, and thumbs, but where are your arms supposed to be? One thing for sure, they should not be held up in the air. They should be resting on the table, or on the quilt that's resting on the table. I usually do most of the control and moving of the quilt with my

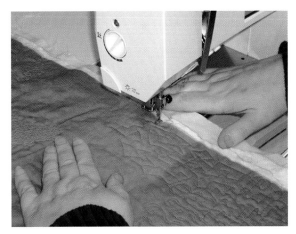
Fig. 1–20. Pressing hands flat.

Fig. 1–21. Hands as a hoop.

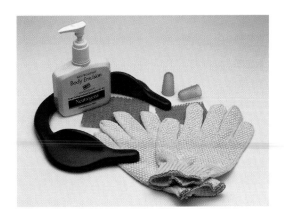
Fig. 1–22. Quilting aids.

Fig. 1–23. Good arm position.

Fig. 1–24. Flapping arms.

Diane's helper, Fluffy.

hands, not my arms. That way my shoulders don't hunch up and get lost up in my ears somewhere. Relax your arms, let them drop to the sewing surface, and find a spot to rest (Fig. 1–23).

Try not to rest any weight on your elbows, however, because constant pressure there will affect the nerve (funny bone) and could cause damage. Rest the underside of your forearms on the sewing table.

AND DON'T FLAP THOSE ELBOWS

If you find you are waving and flapping your elbows as you quilt, the surface is too high, you have had too much caffeine, or you need more time to progress to the next level of machine quilting (Fig. 1–24).

Many machine quilters think that the entire arm is used in moving the quilt. That is sometimes true, of course, and it requires strength in the arms and upper back to handle a heavy quilt. However, just as a small child first uses large motor skills in its development, so do machine quilters. As the child grows and develops, she learns to use fingers and thumb together to do tasks that require fine motor skills. As you progress as a machine quilter, you will do the same thing. You will go from clumsy arm movements to resting your arms on the quilt or cabinet and using your hands and fingers to control the movement of the quilt. This extra control will let you quilt small, fine designs, tiny stippling, and straight lines. Compare it to handwriting. You don't hold your arm up over the desk and move the arm to sign your name. You rest your arm comfortably and use the hand and fingers for writing.

PLAN OF ATTACK

Think of machine quilting as if you were an army general. Mapping out strategies, planning maneuvers, and using your skill and experience are important in planning the quilting for a particular project.

Because machine quilting involves eye-hand-foot coordination, it is best to take advantage of its repetitive nature to reinforce a skill. In other words, doing one motion over and over makes it easier and easier, and the brain can then anticipate the action and go into auto pilot. This is called "muscle memory."

To take advantage of this phenomenon, it is a good idea to do all of one type of quilting throughout the quilt, then the next type, and then the next. For example, do all the walking-foot quilting first to stabilize the quilt, then do all the free-motion quilting. Don't switch back and forth between the walking foot and free-motion.

For free-motion, quilt all the feathers first, then all the grids, then all the background stippling. Make sure there is enough time between techniques for your brain to "re-boot" and switch to the demands of the next technique. Frequent breaks are important, and breaks between types of free-motion quilting are necessary. Many times, it is a good idea to let a night's sleep come between one type and another.

It is also helpful to keep a sample sandwich handy for practicing a style of free-motion quilting until you are loose and comfortable and your brain knows what the pattern is. Even if you are simply following drawn lines, it is a good idea to trace the design on the practice piece and go through it a few times before tackling that design on the quilt. Warm up, loosen up, and you will be much more relaxed, much more confident when you go to the quilt.

Machine quilting is not a buffet where you can choose dessert first. It requires a plan of attack and sticking with it, not jumping around to the "good stuff" whenever you feel like it. Following is a brief summary of the order of quilting that works well.

STABILIZING THE QUILT

If at all possible, look at the quilt layout and find places to stitch in the ditch (straight stitch in the seam lines) to stabilize the entire quilt with an invisible grid of quilting. For instance, in a simple, straight-set block quilt, you can start with the center vertical seam line and quilt between all the vertical rows of blocks, then quilt between all the horizontal rows. If there is sashing, stitch alongside all the sashing seams (Fig. 1–25, page 48). You can do the ditch quilting with a walking foot, but I choose to do it entirely free-motion to eliminate even the slightest possibility of stretching or distorting the quilt top.

If you are working with an on-point block set, quilt all the ditch lines on one diagonal, then the other, always starting somewhere near the center first and working out toward the edges of the quilt (Fig. 1–26, page 48). After the block seams have been stitched, sew the ditch lines between the borders.

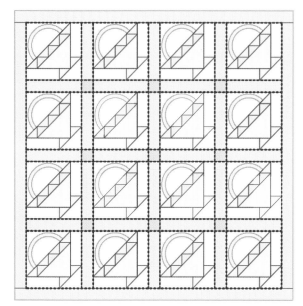

Fig. 1–25. First stabilize your quilt with in-the-ditch quilting.

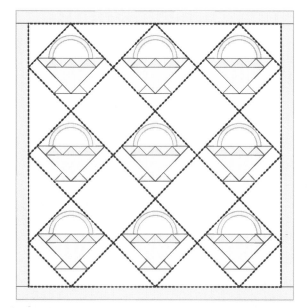

Fig. 1–26. Stabilizing quilting for on-point blocks.

After the quilt has been stabilized with in-the-ditch quilting, many of the pins near these seams can be removed. This lightens the weight and removes obstacles from the remaining quilting. Leave important pins that secure designs yet to be quilted, and leave a few pins to act as little handles for you to hang on to when quilting. These will give you extra control.

Avoid stabilizing by quilting a center vertical seam and then a center horizontal seam. The vertical stitching line puts an obstacle smack dab in the center of every horizontal quilting line that crosses it. Here in Wisconsin, we compare it to plowing snow and reaching a brick wall — the snow just piles up. Quilting all the vertical seams first reduces the amount of fabric that can be pushed along between the seams.

FREE-MOTION DITCH QUILTING

Free-motion ditch quilting is really the same as quilting on a marked line in a design, but you are quilting along a seam line instead. Quilting straight lines takes more concentration than quilting curves, so do this kind of quilting when you are rested, calm, and fresh. Ditch quilting is completely invisible when done carefully (Fig. 1–27).

After the block seams have been stitched in the ditch, free-motion ditch quilting in the interior of the blocks will be the next step in your plan. This too is invisible quilting, and it is the bread and butter of the quilt, the basic stuff that no one will ever see, except on the back.

Don't skip this step for later. The importance of it is to stabilize the sections of the block for further free-motion quilting. It keeps everything in place so you can relax and quilt designs, motifs, and stippling without fear of the layers shifting or the quilt becoming distorted.

FREE-MOTION DESIGNS

Once the quilt has been stabilized, it's time to move out on the highway and do some fancier quilting. Now you can quilt the designs you have traced or the free-motion motifs you want to add to the quilt. The quilt has been stabilized and isn't going any place, so many of the pins can be removed, freeing up space for the fun part of machine quilting, the embellishing.

BACKGROUND QUILTING

It's time to switch mental gears again, take a break, and begin background quilting. This type of quilting can include cross-hatched grids, straight lines, stippling, clamshells, or free-form shapes repeated to fill in an area. Here again, the order of quilting is important. Do the grids, then the lines, then the clamshells in the entire

quilt before the stippling. Stippling is a different type of free-motion quilting requiring greater motor speed and slower hand speed, so it's best to end with it when you are warmed up and relaxed. It will be easier to keep the stippling size and shape consistent if it is done with no backtracking to other kinds of quilting.

It's best to save stippling for last, because it makes the quilt quite stiff and therefore more difficult to work with for other types of quilting. It also draws in the fabric, so quilting straight lines later would be difficult.

Planning ahead, looking down the road, seeing obstacles before they become problems are important in machine quilting. It takes a little thought and work before you even get to the sewing machine, but it pays off in final results and ease of quilting. Make a plan of attack in your head or write down the quilting order to keep track.

Fig. 1–27. A good example of invisible ditch quilting.

THREAD TENSION

What is thread tension? Thread tension refers to how much pressure is placed on the thread as it comes through the machine, either through the top tension disks or through the bobbin case. Thread tension is similar to the tension placed on yarn with your fingers when you are knitting.

Upper Tension

Let's look at the easiest adjustment first. On the upper thread, the tension is usually adjusted with a numbered dial or electronic control. If you are confused about where this adjustment is, consult your owner's manual, which is an important aid when working with your machine. It isn't something to be relegated to the bottom drawer of the cabinet.

A higher number on the tension control indicates more tension on the thread, and a lower number indicates less tension on the thread.

Higher is tighter; lower is looser.

The normal factory tension setting is usually indicated by a line, mark, or arrow. This setting is only a general reference point. It shows you where to set the dial for normal sewing, and the assumption is that you are using the same kind of thread that was used for the initial factory set-up. If you want to use a different type of thread, you will need to change the tension setting. If the stitch doesn't look right, you can adjust the upper tension just a bit and stitch again to see if there is an improvement. Even if your machine has an automatic tension setting, sometimes you can get a much better quality by adjusting the stitch manually.

Remember, the so-called normal setting is arbitrary. On my original sewing machine, I had to keep adjusting the top tension lower and lower. Even when it was at "0," the stitching still did not look right. I took the machine to my repair shop, and the friendly repair man laughed, pulled the dial right off the machine, and put it back on, set at "10". Then I had 10 more stops for lowering it. The number itself is meaningless.

How can you tell if the tension is off? If the top tension is too tight, the line of stitches on top of the quilt will look like a straight piece of thread with little bumps of bobbin thread showing (Fig. 1–28).

To improve the stitch quality, start by lowering the top tension by half a stop. For example, if the dial is set on 5, lower it to 4½.

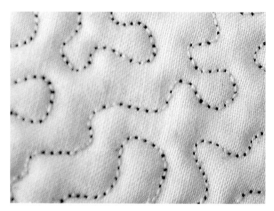

Fig. 1–28. When the tension is too tight, thread from the other side of the quilt pops up to the surface.

Do some test sewing, look at the front and back, and compare it with your previous stitching to see if it is better. Keep lowering the top tension by these small increments until the stitching looks regular with no bobbin thread showing. The back should look similar to the front.

To test thread tension, it helps to use two slightly different colored threads, one in the top, and the other in the bobbin.

CONE-THREAD HOLDER

Nylon monofilament thread and invisible poly thread are more difficult threads to work with to produce quality stitches with proper tension. Even with walking-foot quilting, for which the tension can usually be left at the standard setting, it is necessary to lower the upper tension a small amount for monofilament thread. With free-motion quilting, on many machines, the top tension must be lowered several stops. I have found over the years of quilting with this thread that the best way to control the tension properly is to have the spool of thread completely off the machine and sitting on a cone-thread holder.

In fact, I use a cone-thread holder for all my threads now. The holder is an inexpensive, worth-its-weight-in-gold accessory for sewing and quilting. When the thread is on the holder, it unwinds freely to the loop above the spool, then travels down to the thread guide on the sewing machine where it goes through the tension disks and can be adjusted there. With the cone holder, the thread has a chance to unkink and relax a bit before it goes through the machine. Any loops or twists can be seen as they approach the machine's thread guides and can be smoothed out before they cause all sorts of

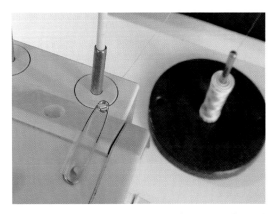

Fig. 1–29. You can add a safety-pin thread guide for extra control. Note the cone-thread holder to the right of the machine.

problems. If needed, you can add control by running the thread through a safety pin taped to your machine (Fig. 1–29). The thread would then go from the holder, through the safety pin, and then through the machine.

If your machine has a horizontal thread spindle, it may be able to handle nylon thread and its tension difficulties just fine. You'll have to work with your set-up and see if the thread gets tangled or snarled, or if it has tight tension that doesn't respond to normal adjustment.

If your machine has a horizontal thread spindle in the top with a lid that closes over it after you thread the machine, it's a good idea to leave the lid open to see if the thread is unwinding correctly. Even with horizontal spindles, it would be better to use a metal cone-thread holder set behind the sewing machine.

BOBBIN TENSION

If you are one of the multitudes of sewing machine owners who cower in fear, break out in hives, or proudly proclaim your refusal to touch the bobbin tension screw, the following information will help you become confident, calm, and adept. You will fearlessly take out the screwdriver that came with your sewing machine and learn to make much needed adjustments to the bobbin tension so that your machine quilting stitch will look as close to perfect as possible.

If the top stitches look perfect but there are bumps of top thread showing on the back and the bobbin thread looks like a straight line, then the bobbin tension is too tight (Fig. 1–30). If the bobbin thread is looped on the back, then the bobbin tension is too loose .

Take heart! Adjusting the bobbin tension is not as scary as everyone has told you. I know your service man has warned you never, under any circumstances, to touch the bobbin setting. However, it is such a simple, straightforward adjustment that anyone can do it successfully with no one the wiser. You need a little screwdriver, and you need to take notes and sew samples, then everything will be fine. You can always set it back the way it was when you started if things don't improve. All the

warnings from the sewing machine shops probably came about because some machine owners made extreme adjustments, then couldn't remember how to adjust the setting back to the way it was.

Take heart! Adjusting the bobbin tension is not as scary as everyone has told you.

One of my students saw that the bobbin tension was too tight, so she took the bobbin out of the machine, whipped out her little screwdriver, and proceeded to unscrew it completely until the screw rolled onto the floor and the case fell apart. Even in this severe case, we were able to put the case back together and adjust the bobbin tension until we had a perfect line of stitches. She was entirely too "gung ho" with her adjusting. You needn't be quite that rambunctious.

Like the upper-tension dial, the general rule of thumb is to turn the screw to the right to tighten the tension and to the left to loosen it. The adjusting screw is usually on the outside of the bobbin case. If your

Fig. 1-30. Bobbin tension is too tight, so the top thread is being drawn the the back. The loops of thread (bird's nest) are caused by not holding the threads as you start to sew.

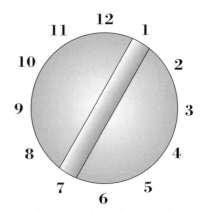

Fig. 1-31. To remember where the bobbin tension started, you can think of the bobbin screw as a clock face.

machine doesn't have a bobbin case and the bobbin sits directly in the machine, there is usually a screw centered in front of the bobbin housing. The housing can't be removed like a bobbin case, but the little screw still controls how tight or loose the bobbin tension is.

To adjust the bobbin tension, think of the screw head as a clock face and the indentation for the screwdriver as the pointer on the clock (Fig. 1–31). Before making any adjustments, draw a picture on a note pad of how the "clock" is set, for example, one o'clock. Then if the tension is too tight, you will loosen the screw by turning it to the left. Turn it half a stop to a point between noon and one o'clock. Sew a sample line of stitches and check the back to see how they look. If the changed setting made no improvement, loosen the screw to noon and sew another line of stitches. Keep loosening the screw and checking the stitches until the tension is correct. Each machine adjusts differently. Some respond immediately to small changes, and some take several stops on the clock face to show improvement.

If the stitches on the back show as loops, you will do the reverse and tighten the screw by turning it to the right. If nothing good happens to your stitches as you test your adjustments, you can always return the bobbin tension screw to its original position and try something else.

If you see problems on the quilt back (usually too-tight bobbin tension) only from time to time or in a certain direction during free-motion quilting, then using the single-hole throat plate may help keep the bobbin stitches straight and even.

If you really cannot do much with your stitch quality or uneven tension, then it's definitely time for a visit to the service center for a check-up. Make sure that you sew some samples and mark them clearly with the settings you used. Include the samples with the machine so the repair person can see what the problem is. Also, take some of the thread you normally use and have him adjust the tension for your thread sewn on two pieces of your quilt-quality cotton rather than their usual sample fabric.

LOG CABIN REVISITED, 86" x 86". This "sacrifice" quilt was used to learn a new sewing machine. (Cotton Classic® batt, nylon monofilament thread, original trapunto quilting in the border.)

WALKING-FOOT QUILTING

The walking foot is an aid for machine quilters that helps move the top layer of the quilt sandwich along at the same rate as the bottom layer, preventing pleats, stretching, and distortion (Fig. 1–32). It is a great tool for beginners to use in learning how to handle the bulk and the layers of a big quilt because the sewing machine does so much of the work for them.

When using the walking foot, you need to package and prepare the quilt for the sewing machine, secure it so that it will fit through the arm of the machine, and support it and feed it through the machine during quilting (Fig. 1–33).

For the first two years that I machine quilted, using the walking foot was my only method of quilting. My sewing machine was old and had problems, making free-motion quilting something that was all but impossible to do. So I pieced and quilted a project each month by using the walking foot to do straight-line quilting. The quilts looked wonderful, and after working with this foot for so long, I learned its possibilities as well as its limitations.

The foot has either metal or synthetic feed dogs that correspond to those on the sewing machine. The foot also has an arm that fits over or around the thumb screw holding the needle. When the machine makes a stitch and the needle moves up and down, the walking-foot arm moves with it. The arm is connected to the walking foot's feed dogs, which then move the

Fig. 1–32. Walking foot.

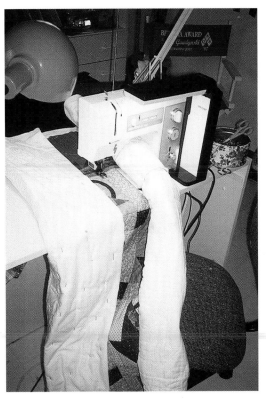

Fig. 1–33. Packaging a quilt for machine quilting.

fabric along in time with the feed dogs in the machine. Generic walking feet do not work properly on all machines. Try to get a foot that is made by the manufacturer of your sewing machine.

The walking foot is a wonderful tool for introducing yourself to the pleasures of machine quilting because it does the work for you. The stitch length is set on the sewing machine, and the feed dogs and the walking foot move the quilt along at the correct rate to create the stitch length. With a walking foot, you are only the guide, the quilt holder-upper, the manager, the pinner, and un-pinner. You simply do everything you can to allow the machine to do its job easily and correctly.

Straight quilting lines show on busy print fabrics. As a simple beginning technique for a print border, especially a busy floral, use the walking foot to quilt parallel lines around the border. The distance between the lines can be the width of the walking foot. There's no marking, it's easy to quilt, and it gives a lovely textured effect that is clearly visible.

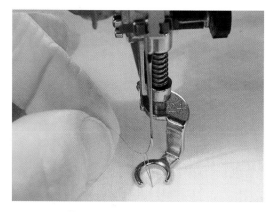

Fig. 1–34. Bringing the bobbin thread to the surface.

Starting and Stopping

It is vital that the line of stitching be secured adequately so it doesn't come out and so it doesn't show. Simple backstitching of one or two stitches does not hold well. Letting the needle go up and down several times in the same hole does not hold the stitching. Instead, a knot of thread builds up on the back, which is obvious and unsightly.

Many of the new machines have a lock stitch. These work fine for normal sewing and piecing, but they are quite noticeable in quilting. The lock stitch should not be used unless you can experiment with it to create a secure start and stop that are not obvious. For those machines that do not have a short enough stitch-length adjustment, the locking feature may be your only alternative.

TO QUILT A ROW OF STITCHING WITH THE WALKING FOOT, FOLLOW THESE STEPS:

• **Place the needle** directly over the starting point and lower the presser foot.

• **Take one stitch**, making sure it is complete; that is, the needle has returned to its highest position.

• **Holding the top thread** and with the presser foot down, give the thread a gentle tug to pull a loop of bobbin thread to the top of the quilt (Fig. 1–34). With both threads on top of the quilt, they will not get quilted in on the back.

• **When you begin stitching,** hold on to these two threads firmly but gently because you don't want to bend the needle. Holding the threads will also prevent loops and "bird's nests" from forming on the back (Figs. 1–30, page 52).

• **Set the stitch length** to slightly above "0" or at the buttonhole symbol. The stitches should be about a needle's width apart, not on top of each other, but very close together. Take seven or eight of these tiny stitches to lock in a row of quilting.

• **Change the stitch length** one number up, take one or two stitches, then move it up another number and take several more stitches. Continue moving the number up until you reach the desired stitch length. This entire step from very small to normal-size stitches should be no more than about one inch. It usually takes me two or three stitch-length adjustments to reach the final size I use for the entire line of quilting (Fig. 1–35).

If you have an electronic machine, check with your dealer or your owner's manual to see if there is a way to program this stitch length change into your machine's memory. Then one setting would automatically provide you with securing stitches.

• **Stitch the row of quilting,** then start decreasing the stitch length about one inch from the end of the row. At the last one-fourth inch, you will be taking the tiniest possible stitches to finish the row.

• **If you forget and quilt** all the way to the end of the row, stop, set the stitch length indicator to the shortest stitch setting (the one you used to begin the row), and using reverse, stitch back over the line of quilting for seven or eight stitches to secure the row.

• **Lift the presser foot,** clip the top thread right at the quilt surface, then turn the quilt over and clip the thread on the back. This is a good time to inspect the back of the quilt to make sure the stitch quality is good, and you haven't quilted in anything from the floor of your sewing room.

As you pull the quilt back toward you to start the next row of stitching, remove any pins that are no longer needed.

Managing the Quilt

The quilt needs to be supported at all times when you are quilting. You need to have it rolled on the right side and folded or arranged on the left. You need support to the left and to the back to catch and hold the weight of the quilt while you feed it through the machine.

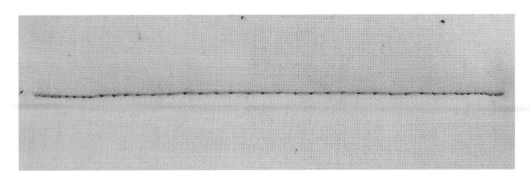

Fig. 1–35. When starting a line of stitching, change the stitch length gradually.

Do not pull the quilt toward you. Some of my students have had the idea that pulling the quilt will keep it flat and pucker-free, but it will actually stretch and distort the quilt. It will also fight the feed dogs.

One of my students was certain that her machine was broken, because no matter what setting was used for the stitch-length indicator, even the largest basting size, the resulting stitches were tiny and closely spaced. She thought it was "stuck" on the setting from those first stitches. As I watched her, I could see she was pulling the quilt tight toward herself, making the walking foot "spin its wheels." I set the stitch length to the proper setting, supported the quilt, and fed it down to the needle with no pulling and no weight on it. It sewed a perfect row of stitches, the exact length used on the setting.

To control a large quilt, I place it in the machine with the bulk of it on the floor to

my left. I pull most of the quilt onto my lap and then up under my chin (Fig. 1–36). From this position (hot!), I feed the quilt down to the machine. This way, there is no pull or drag on the quilt, and its weight is being supported by me. My hands guide the quilt in the machine, and the foot makes the stitches.

Some quilters prefer to roll the quilt and place it over the shoulder so it feeds down to the needle from a height, but this is uncomfortable for me. Try it several ways and decide what is the best method for you. Whatever you do, the important thing is to keep the weight of the quilt off the area that is going under the needle.

ALL-OVER GRID QUILTING

When you use a walking foot, it is possible to quilt a cross-hatched grid over the entire surface of the quilt, from edge to edge. This is a fast, efficient, and almost fool-proof method for machine quilting a simple yet effective traditional design and turning one of your many tops into a real quilt quickly. My first quilts were done this way, and I could pin the quilt one day and quilt one-fourth of the lines each day. Then I could bind and complete the quilt, wash it, and have it on my bed within a week.

Even with a sewing machine that had its problems, these quilts turned out nicely. Any pulling of the fabric between the quilting lines was minimized by the shrinkage of the batt after the quilt was washed. I did use monofilament nylon thread because I was quilting over many different fabrics, but a neutral taupe cotton would have also worked well. Sometimes, it may be necessary to mark the quilting lines, but often you can let the piecing provide you with the ditches and guides needed to quilt a top quickly.

Fig. 1–36. Feeding a large quilt into the machine.

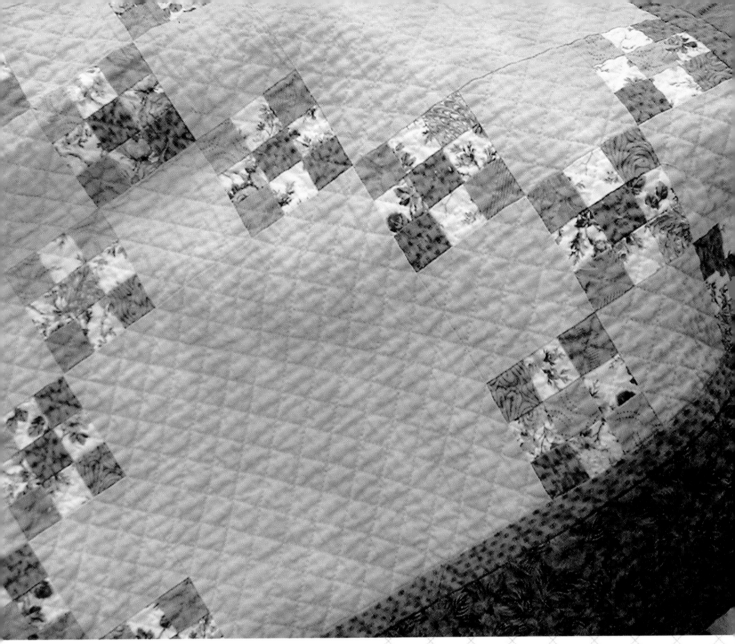

Fig. 1-37. This Double Nine-Patch is a handsome example of all-over grid quilting.

For an all-over grid quilt, the trick is to use a small grid, with lines less than two inches apart. If you use a cotton batt and wash the quilt when you are finished, it will shrink up a bit and give it an heirloom look. Many old quilts were done in this simple manner, and they look strikingly beautiful (Fig. 1–37).

Grid Quilting a Large Quilt

DIAGONAL SETTING

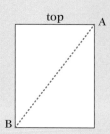

Stitch the first row from A to B through the center.

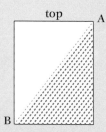

Stitch the rows from the center out to the lower-right corner.

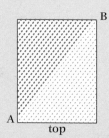

Turn the quilt top to bottom. Re-package the quilt and sew from the center out to the lower-right corner. The whole quilt is now "channel quilted."

Rotate the quilt as shown and re-package it. Again, stitch from the center out to the lower-right corner.

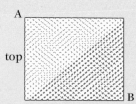

Turn the quilt top to bottom and re-package it. Stitch from the center to the lower-right corner.

STRAIGHT SETTING

Quilt the long vertical center line first.

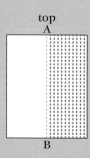

Then quilt all the lines to the right of the center one.

Turn the quilt top to bottom and quilt all the remaining vertical lines out to the right edge.

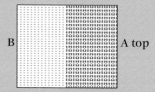

After all the vertical lines have been quilted, rotate the quilt and quilt a center line and all the lines to the right, out to the edge of the quilt.

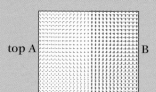

Turn the quilt top to bottom and quilt the last quadrant from the center outward.

FREQUENT WALKING-FOOT QUESTIONS

Q: Why do I get various stitch lengths when using the walking foot? I thought the stitch length was programmed.

A: A walking foot cannot pull the quilt off the floor and through the machine – it isn't that strong. You need to support the quilt, hold and lift it, and smooth it out gently as it approaches the needle so there is no weight or drag on the needle.

Many quilters think that, to get a flat quilt with no pleats and puckers, it is necessary to put tension on the quilt as it goes through the machine. They play tug of war with the quilt, and the poor walking foot can't possibly move the quilt along when you are pulling it (Fig. 1–38). The result is uneven or very small stitches.

Another tell-tale sign of an overly aggressive pilot is the presence of gouges or burrs on the opening in the throat plate. If you pull on the quilt while it is going through the machine, you may actually bend the needle. When the needle enters the quilt at an angle, it will nick the edge of the opening in the throat plate. I have seen many machines with throat plate openings that closely resemble the way a spoon looks when it has been dropped in a garbage disposal.

A damaged throat plate will cause immense difficulty for you when you switch to free-motion quilting because the thread will continually get caught in the burrs, causing tension problems, fraying, or breakage.

The solution is to replace the throat plate or have it filed down, and remember not to pull on the quilt.

Q: Do I need to mark the straight lines I will be quilting with my walking foot?

A: Sometimes yes, sometimes no. Many of the newer walking feet come with a guide that rides on a previously stitched line so the line you are quilting will be the correct distance away from the previous one (Fig. 1–39). Using the guide takes some practice and a good eye for looking at one thing while quilting another.

Many times, in a pieced quilt, it is easy to eyeball a straight line from one point to the next without having to mark it. If the distance becomes too great, however, then it is definitely a good idea to mark a line to

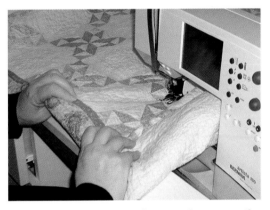

Fig. 1–38. Playing tug of war with your quilts will cause uneven or tiny stitches.

Fig. 1–39. Stitching guide for sewing grids.

follow. It is definitely obvious when quilted lines wobble and waiver when they are supposed to be straight. With practice, however, you will become much better at sewing a straight line with no marking.

Q: Should I cut out the metal front of my walking foot for better visibility?

A: Yes, you can try cutting out the front of your walking foot to improve visibility. Many new walking feet have open toes, which really provide super visibility. They are especially helpful when pulling up the bobbin thread or starting and stopping a line of stitching. I used my old walking foot without removing the metal bar with no problems, but the new open-toed ones are wonderful.

Q: My walking foot is generic and seems to make the quilting look worse than when I don't use it.

A: It is best to get a walking foot that is made for your machine, if possible. A generic foot is a stop-gap measure, or a last resort if your make or model of machine does not have a walking foot available from the manufacturer. However, many of the walking feet are wobbly, don't fit correctly, and they sometimes even fall apart with use.

I have seen some generic walking feet that have such a small opening for the needle that, when the machine is in use and things move and jiggle, the needle hits the opening every time. Some feet have feed dogs that are so hard and brittle they leave little "tire marks" on the quilt that even washing won't remove.

Q: Why can't I quilt the first line from top to bottom then quilt the second line from the bottom up to the top, rather than cutting the thread and pulling the quilt through the machine and starting back up at the top?

A: Sewing from the bottom to the top on the second row is exactly what you would do in free-motion quilting. However, with a walking foot and feed dogs, you would have to turn the entire quilt around, and you cannot turn a big rolled-up quilt in the sewing machine.

My grid lines are usually done with free-motion quilting so that I can do them quickly and efficiently. Rather than stopping and starting with each line of quilting, with free-motion, I can quilt sideways to the next line and then backward up to the top again, then sideways and down (Fig. 1–40).

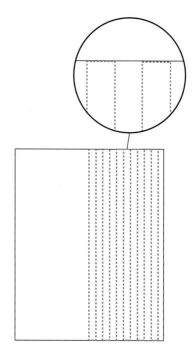

Fig. 1-40. With free-motion quilting, you can quilt sideways to the next line and back up to the top without stopping.

Q: Sometimes, when I put the walking foot on the machine, it won't work at all, and it even seems that the needle is hitting something solid in the bobbin area. What did I do wrong?

A: You probably forgot to put the little arm of the walking foot over or around the thumb screw assembly. It has to be engaged and working for the foot to sew properly (Fig. 1–41). Otherwise you will get no feed-dog action, or the problem you describe. Take the walking foot off and reattach it and see if that helps.

Fig. 1–41. Be sure the walking foot arm is over or around the thumb screw for the needle.

BUTTERNUT SUMMER, 81" x 81". This quilt was made as a tribute to my father after his death. It includes motifs in the quilting that remind me of him. (Many original quilting designs, including the border feathers. Trapunto, nylon monofilament thread, Cotton Classic® batt. Winner of the Bernina Award for Machine Workmanship at the American Quilters Society Quilt Show, and in the MAQS permanent collection.)

FREE-MOTION QUILTING

Sewing with a presser foot and feed dogs is like running a train on tracks. You have to stay on the tracks, and you can sew only forward or in reverse. You cannot stitch sideways or make loops and curls. You can do some of these things with the walking foot on a very small quilt, because you can turn the quilt the small amount needed to accommodate minimal direction changes. But if you have a piece larger than about 30 inches, it is too difficult to be turning it constantly.

Sometimes, the most difficult concept to convey to someone unfamiliar with a technique is the simplest one, the cornerstone of the whole process – free-motion quilting was devised so you can quilt a big quilt in a small machine with something other than straight lines. It allows you to quilt loops and spirals in any direction you want *without turning the quilt.*

Along Came Harriet

When I first heard Harriet Hargrave give her lecture on machine quilting, I was only half paying attention, because I knew I could machine quilt small pieces. The walking foot made that possible, but it was ditch quilting – just quilting in the seam lines. That was the type of machine quilting most of us were doing back in the 1980s, and we were not very proud of it. The most elaborate design that was possible was a simple cable in the border. Because the lines were gentle and wavy, they could be done "on the railroad tracks," with minimal turning of the quilt. Then I saw Harriet's quilts! Designs! Feathers! Stippling! Echoes! Continuous curves! A glorious feast for a starved quilter's eyes. How in the world did she do that? All was made clear in her presentation, and the light bulb went on in my head.

Beginning Free-Motion

Many years and many quilts later, I realize it is still this simple idea that is the basis of all free-motion quilting: lower the feed dogs, quilt in any direction. Some of my students fully believe that having to move the quilt, run the machine, and stay on a marked design is just an ingenious method of torture I have devised for them. They have little thought balloons over their heads saying, "Doesn't she know you can use feed dogs, and they make it so much easier to get even stitches?"

To counteract the attitude of non-belief, I have students bring a 36-by-40-inch quilt sandwich for practicing. They have to roll it up and manipulate the bulk, so it's not easy to turn the quilt when following a design. In fact, it's impossible, especially in the limited space of a classroom. Some students may still think it is just a form of torture, but for others, the light bulb goes on instantly. "Oh, you have to stitch sideways! The roll of the quilt makes a nice handle! So you don't turn the quilt to go over there, you keep it facing you and just stitch in any direction you want! Way cool!"

I hope you will pin a lap-sized quilt together and try some free-motion quilting on it to understand the freedom of sewing in any direction.

Someone once described the technique of free-motion quilting as drawing a picture with a pen that is held stationary in a vise. You then hold the paper under the pen and move the paper in any direction to make your drawing.

Set the stitch length to zero when doing free-motion quilting. Even though it can't affect the stitch length, it keeps the feed dogs from moving, saving a lot of unnecessary wear and tear on your machine.

FEED DOGS

The first marketed sewing machines in the 1800s did not have feed dogs. A sewer back then had to move the fabric through the machine herself. If her speed of moving the fabric was even and coordinated with the treadle speed, her stitches were even. If she was a bit hasty or impatient and moved the fabric too fast, she produced large, uneven stitches. If she was slow, unsure, and hesitant and moved the fabric too slowly, her stitches piled up on one another, and knots formed on the back. She

also likely created "bird's nests" on the back. This is the same thing that happens now when we take our modern electronic machines, with memory and every form of setting you could imagine, and deliberately disable the one mechanism that those early sewers would have done anything to have, the feed dogs.

It's no wonder it is so difficult to convince students, with their expensive, electronic machines, that they need only the basics from their machine to do the most beautiful and intricate quilting:

- **Good speed control.**

- **Good tension** for needle and bobbin threads.

- **Lowered feed dogs.**

- **Free-motion foot** with good clearance.

SPEED

Speed is something you will have to work out for yourself. Some quilters believe that, if you run the machine very fast, the stitches will be more even, but some people are not comfortable with that amount of speed. You can do free-motion quilting successfully at any speed, even stitch by stitch. You will have to experiment and try various speeds to see what is right for you.

Speed correlates with personality, and to tell everyone to quilt fast or slow doesn't take into consideration our comfort levels.

It's important to realize that all speeds are used in machine quilting. Stippling requires a faster speed than feathers do.

You need to slow down for double stitching so the second line will be undetectable. When you realize that it is okay to go faster some times and slower at others, you will start understanding that the finesse you seek will come with learning to control all the variables.

If machine quilting has left you feeling out of control, I hope you will try it again, only this time you might try slowing down. Once you feel that you are in the driver's seat, your comfort and relaxation will be reflected in much improved quilting.

WARM-UPS

For successful free-motion quilting, it is really important to be warmed up and relaxed. A good way to loosen up is to keep a practice or "warm-up" sandwich ready at all times. Use it for a few minutes before you start quilting on an actual project. Usually a 10-minute warm-up is plenty to get you used to the thread you will be using and the design you will be doing for real. You can check the tension and make any adjustments as well.

I vary my grip between holding and lifting the quilt and using my palms when necessary. There is definitely a knack to holding the quilt taut like an embroidery hoop and, at the same time, moving it at a speed in rhythm with the machine's speed, which you are controlling with your foot. Learning this technique will take practice, and the warm-up will get you coordinated. It really helps if you can rest your arms on the cabinet so you don't have to worry about doing all of this and, at the same time, holding your arms up in the air.

FOR YOUR WARM-UP, TRY THE FOLLOWING EXERCISES WITH THE FEED DOGS LOWERED:

1. Near the center of the practice quilt, bring up a loop of bobbin thread.

• **Lower the presser foot.**

• **Take one complete stitch.** The needle will be all the way up at the start of the stitch and at the end.

• **Give the top thread a gentle tug** and pull a loop of the bobbin thread to the top of the quilt (see Fig. 1–34, page 56).

2. Hold these two threads with one hand and take four or five very closely spaced stitches to secure the line of stitching. Do this by moving the quilt very slowly while you are stitching.

3. Stitch a line toward yourself, moving the quilt at about the rate you would if you were sewing with a walking foot and feed dogs. If the stitches are too large, you are moving the quilt too fast. If the stitches are all cramped and piled up on one another, you aren't moving the quilt at all. You have to loosen up your muscles, move the quilt evenly, and run the machine at a medium speed. If you go too slow, you may break needles. If you go too fast, you may lose accuracy. Experiment!

4. Stitch about a four-inch line toward yourself, stitch sideways to the right, then stitch backward in a straight line. When you change directions, you will get a nice clean corner if you hesitate a moment before proceeding in a new direction.

It might help to place a dot where you want the line of stitching to end. Then look at the dot and stitch to it. Don't look at the needle or the presser foot.

5. Continue with these straight lines until you feel more relaxed and the stitches begin to look more even.

6. Now it's time to loosen up even more and do some loops and curves. Try "drawing" simple shapes like clouds, leaves, and flowers as you quilt.

7. Quilt your signature.

8. Try some spirals.

9. Once you feel you have loosened up and relaxed, try following a marked design for your next lesson. With a marked design, you will have to do all of the above, but stay on the line as well.

SOME THINGS TO REMEMBER:

• **Look ahead** of the needle.

• **Let your arms relax** and rest on the machine.

• **Look up** every now and then and stop to rest your eyes. Focus on something across the room, and every 30 minutes or so, close your eyes completely for a minute or two.

• **Do some stretches;** get up and walk around.

• **Breathe!**

Curves are the easiest and most forgiving shapes to quilt. You can use simple loops, all connected to one another, as an overall quilting design on a busy print. You will have lovely texture and dimension, and you will not have any markings to remove. On a busy print, a marked design wouldn't show up anyway.

Quilting a Marked Design

When I first tried to follow a marked design, I was barely able to move my hands and run the machine at the same time. If I sped up the machine, I moved my hands faster too. At other times, it felt like my hands were mired in glue and wouldn't move at all. I sat helplessly, watching the machine speed the needle in and out, forming piles of little stitches going nowhere.

Let's go through the quilting of a marked design, with some advice and information, so your first experience can be more enjoyable than mine was.

CHOOSING A DESIGN

The problems encountered by most beginners on their first try are frequently caused by design choice. Sometimes the simplest designs are the most difficult to quilt, and the more complex-looking designs are much easier.

LOOK FOR THE FOLLOWING FEATURES IN A QUILTING DESIGN:

• **Small curvy shapes,** like a wreath with small feathers.

• **Designs without straight lines.** It's much more difficult to free-motion quilt a straight line than a curvy one.

• **Designs without parallel lines.** Parallel lines are even more difficult. It's immediately apparent to the eye if two lines are not straight and parallel.

• **Designs no larger than 6" to 8"** to start with. Larger designs may have long smooth

areas to quilt, so they are more difficult. Also, you will have to move the quilt around a lot more.

• **A continuous-line design** made for machine quilting, rather than a traditional hand-quilting design, like a feathered wreath or rope border (Fig. 1–42).

• **A motif with more connecting lines** rather than fewer. It will be easier to quilt because the lines are shorter, and you can control the quilt much more easily with less hand movement.

• **An obvious design path.** If you can't for the life of you see where to proceed in the design, it can be frustrating. Some designs come with arrows or numbers to show you the way.

MAKING A SAMPLE

• **Trace a design** on a 15" muslin fabric square. Give yourself several inches of space at the edge for your "handle," so you have something to grip and hold firm with your hands while quilting.

• **Connect the gaps** if you have used a stencil to trace the design (Fig. 1–43). Taking a few minutes to connect the lines to form one solid line will help you quilt smooth lines.

• **Pin baste close enough** to the design lines to keep them from shifting during quilting but not so close as to hit the presser foot (Fig. 1–44). It's annoying and causes irregular quilting if you either hit a pin or have to stop to move or remove one. Plan ahead. Many times, when pinning closely around designs, I use the smaller #1 safety pins.

QUILTING THE DESIGN

• **Where to begin?** If yours is a continuous-line design that is numbered, the design

a.

b.

Fig. 1–42. (a) Continuous-line design. (b) Hand quilting design.

Fig. 1–43. Fill in the gaps left by a stencil.

will tell you where to begin. A good place to start is usually the center or somewhere near the center. One of the first designs I quilted was started at one side, and by the time I quilted to the other side I had managed to snowplow extra fabric over there (it wasn't pinned enough) and ended up with a pleat quilted in.

• **Do one area,** one shape of the design at a time. It's okay to stop, shake your hands, look up and blink, rest your eyes, and reposition your hands for a better grip. Try to stop for that break at a good point in the design where the stop and start place won't be noticeable.

• **Use needle-down** when you stop, if you have that feature on your machine. If you don't, when you stop during the quilting of the design, turn the wheel on the machine to lower the needle into the quilt. The free-motion foot does not touch the surface of the quilt and won't clamp it in place like a walking foot or a regular presser foot would do.

• **Before resuming quilting,** bring the needle to the fully up position to keep it from pulling on the quilt and causing that first

stitch to jump off the line. Be aware that stopping and starting are where most of the uneven stitches occur.

• **As you approach the end** of the design where you will connect with your starting point, gradually decrease the speed of your hands, making the stitches progressively smaller, until you meet those first stitches. Sew over one or two of them to lock in the line of stitching. Clip your thread on the top, then turn the quilt over and cut the bobbin thread at the quilt, leaving no tails.

• **Keep your sample as a reference.** Stitch around the outside edge of the practice sandwich to secure the edges. Wash the sample in cool water to remove the blue marks, and let it dry, or dry it in the dryer for more shrinkage and an old-fashioned look.

• **Analyze the problems** you had when you quilted the sample to see if they show now that it is finished. Chances are, if you chose a design that was appropriate to your skill level and followed the instructions, it will look very nice.

Keep in mind that, when you choose this same design to place on an actual quilt and repeat it perhaps 20 or more times over an entire quilt top, your skill will increase dramatically each time you go around the design.

For my first try at free-motion designs, I pieced a small lap quilt for practice only. I knew it was only to learn to machine quilt, but I tried to do the best I could. The first few designs were wobbly, uneven, off-kilter. By the time I had finished the top, I could do a very good continuous-line design. If you want to perfect this skill, you must

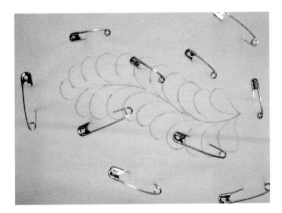

Fig. 1–44. Pinned feather design, ready for quilting.

actually make quilts. No one wants to waste time and materials on samples or practice pieces until the skill has been learned. When I look at those early quilts, they are lovely and I still use them. On close inspection they will provide some laughs at their awkward stitches and simple skill level, but I have progressed from those to do the kind of quilts I could only dream about then.

ROSES FOR JOAN, 36" x 34½". Made by Joan Botsford. Layered with Hobbs Heirloom® batting, the wallhanging was quilted with nylon monofilament thread. This was the quilt-maker's first attempt at trapunto, free-hand feathers, and tiny stippling.

Echo Quilting

Once you are comfortable with the feel and coordination of moving the quilt under the needle, keeping the quilt smooth and taut with your hands, and varying the speed of the machine to coordinate with the speed of your hands, it is time for you to try some echo quilting. Like many other skills, machine quilting can be broken down into building blocks, or skill levels, that lead to more complex techniques. Echo quilting is the basic free-motion technique that, once mastered, will allow you to achieve all sorts of wonderful machine artistry skills (Fig. 1–45). It is the foundation for all other machine quilting skills, and if you learn it, you will be able to do stippling and feathers as well as free-hand designs with ease.

What is echo quilting? If you are familiar with Hawaiian-style quilting, you will immediately recognize this technique. It has several important components:

- There is no marking.

- **It outlines another** quilting design, pieced work, or appliqué.

- **It repeats** the shape it surrounds, over and over, until a natural finishing point is reached; for example, a seam, the next part of the quilt, or the outside edge.

- **The design can become more indefinite** with each round, or it can precisely mirror the shape right out to the edge.

- **The lines may be spaced evenly** or unevenly as in a grass-cloth look.

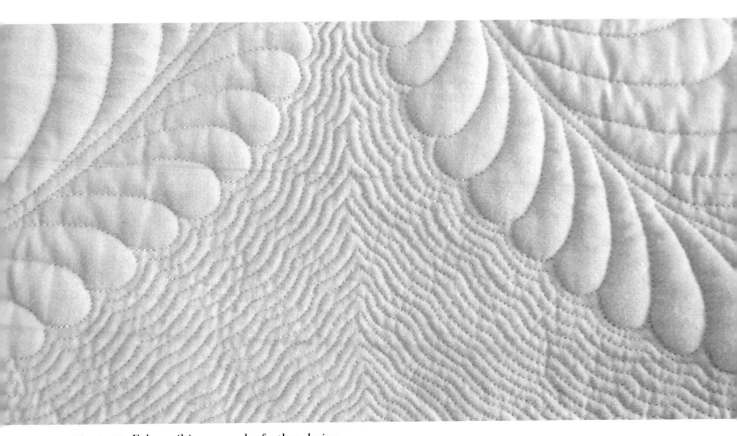

Fig. 1–45. Echo quilting around a feather design.

• It easily creates wonderful background quilting.

• Great secondary designs can occur where two areas of echo quilting merge.

Why echo quilting? It teaches all the necessary elements of control, spacing, stitch length, where to look, and even how to handle a large, heavy quilt. Learning to echo quilt will prepare you for stippling, quilting marked continuous-line designs, and more complex skills, like stitching free-motion grids or feathers.

When echo quilting, you will have to learn to position the quilt under the needle so there is no drag on it and be able to move it along smoothly with no resistance. The moment you start echoing with no feed dogs, you will realize that there is a certain amount of shifting the quilt and repositioning that you will have to do to keep the stitches even and the quilt's movement unrestricted. I usually call this technique "nesting" or "puddling" the quilt (Fig. 1–46).

Picture putting a pile of mashed potatoes on your plate and making an indentation where the gravy lake goes. This is exactly what you do with a quilt — mound it up around the needle to make a gravy lake!

Because the quilt is dammed up all around the area you are quilting, you will be able to move this small lake area easily. As soon as you feel resistance or pull on the quilt and you can't move it freely, re-position the "potatoes" so you can continue. After a while, you will do this without even thinking.

Stop running the machine while you reposition your hands or the quilt. Use the needle-down feature when you stop because it will keep the work steady, exactly at the point where you stopped. Remember to raise the needle to the up position before resuming quilting.

Echo quilting teaches spacing. This is the basis of many free-motion techniques,

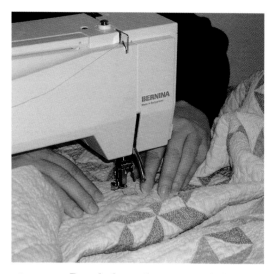

Fig. 1–46. Bunch the quilt up around the needle, leaving a small "puddle" area.

Fig. 1–47. Keep the edge of the foot on the previous line of quilting.

including stippling. Where do you look? How do you judge the distance? Usually a good point to look at is the edge of the foot you are using. When the first row of echo quilting has been stitched, the edge of the foot, or a point on the foot if it is larger than a quarter inch, should just touch the edge of the design you are going around (Fig. 1–47). Then for each subsequent row, the edge of the foot will touch the line of stitching just completed, and voila! You have just taught yourself one of the most important concepts in every single type of free-motion quilting. Do not look at the needle!

Because echo quilting forces you to look, most of the time, at the line you have previously stitched, you get into the habit of not looking at the needle. As you become more proficient at echo quilting, you can vary the distance between lines so you don't have to use the presser foot as your guide. You can estimate any amount of space, and this ability to space lines is invaluable.

Stitch length is easy to learn when echo quilting because you forget to think about it. You are so busy trying to control the weight of the quilt and space the lines that the double whammy of coordinating foot control (motor) speed with hand movement is momentarily put on the back burner. When you actually relax and quit agonizing over how fast you should go and settle down and think spacing, it starts happening naturally. Also, with echo quilting, you don't have the added burden of trying to stay on a marked design.

To learn echo quilting, make the following practice piece. In a quilt border, mark a simple quilt design, like a cable or oak leaves, or even a simple feathered vine. Then echo quilt around it. You can quilt the entire border in two continuous lines, one on each side of the design (Fig. 1–48).

When echo quilting around a design, always start on the outside line of the design being echoed. Use small stitches to lock in your quilting, then veer out into the space around the design about one-fourth inch. As you go around the entire design and approach the starting point, you will see that you will automatically keep spiraling around with no need to stop and start each round.

When doing echo quilting on borders, it is important to first stay-stitch the outside edge of the quilt (through all three layers) about one-eighth inch in from the raw edge. I do this with a walking foot or use free-motion so as not to stretch the edge of the quilt. Then, as you do the echo quilting, pleats or tucks won't occur as you push the fabric along.

Use echo quilting inside a design. Echo quilting can be used to give some definition to the inside of a quilting design, such as a large circle or flower. It is also used in

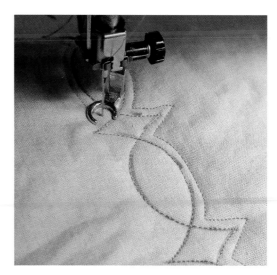

Fig. 1–48. Make a practice piece for echo quilting.

Fig. 1–49. Echo quilting inside an appliqué design.

Fig. 1–50. Echo-quilted doodle.

appliqué pieces so they do not have to be marked for quilting. Sometimes the echo is only one line, so it is similar to the outline quilting that hand quilters do on appliqué pieces. Sometimes the echoing fills the entire shape with quilting (Fig. 1–49).

Echo-quilt motifs. A great way to doodle designs in a given area on a quilt without marking them is to use the echo technique. You might like to try the following practice piece: Stitch a simple shape, such as a spiral, leaf, star, or flower. Spiral out and around the shape and echo it several times. Add new shapes that contrast with the first, like loops, spikes, peaks, and scallops, then echo these shapes. Keep building shapes and echoing them, keeping the spacing between all the quilting lines consistent. The area will be filled with wonderful quilting, all based on echoing simple shapes you can quilt without marking (Fig. 1–50).

One of the best features of echo quilting is that you do not have to mark it. If the spacing isn't perfect, it doesn't matter.

KETTLE MORAINE STAR, 90" x 90". This star was inspired by old Amish and Mennonite Lone Star quilts. It is made with a Cotton Classic® batt, nylon monofilament thread, and trapunto. The star is quilted in the continuous curve technique. (1997 Bernina Award for Machine Workmanship and part of the permanent MAQS collection.)

Continuous Curves

When I first began to machine quilt and use free-motion skills, I wondered how I could do traditional outline quilting yet have the line continue from one area to the next. It's the stopping and starting, cutting thread, taking small stitches, etc., that is so time consuming in machine quilting. I always say to myself, "If I could do this faster by hand, then I am doing something wrong."

Outline quilting is the time-honored way to hand quilt small shapes and patches in blocks, but for machine quilting, it needs to be done without all the stopping and starting. Continuous curves is a technique that does just that. It mimics the look of outline quilting, but the stitching line is made up of connected curves, eliminating all the stopping and starting and cutting the threads (Fig. 1–51).

Here are some of the reasons to learn this valuable technique:

• **It is a no-mark method,** although you can use the width of your free-motion foot as a guide to determine how far to curve outward, which reduces time.

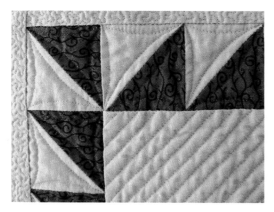

Fig. 1-51. Continuous-curve quilting of half-square triangles in a sawtooth border.

• **The curves connect** one shape or part of a block to the next, and that saves an amazing amount of time because there is minimal stopping and starting.

• **It takes quilting out of the ditch** and puts it on the surface of the quilt where it will show, giving the quilt a much more intensely quilted look. The technique makes a quilt look more like a hand-quilted one.

• **It is easy.** Even beginners can learn it right away. With some walking-foot quilting to stabilize the quilt and a few free-motion designs suitable for a beginner, add some continuous curve quilting, and a first quilt will look very nice, very professional, very non-beginner.

• **It is suitable for many applications.** Use it to quilt an entire quilt, such as a Lone Star, or individual blocks or borders. You can even quilt a background if you mark a grid, do the curves, and then remove the marking.

• **Mistakes are unnoticeable.** Curves that are slightly different from one another don't show. The overall effect minimizes any variations that occur within the curves.

• **You will become competent** very quickly, with repetition. A quilter told me she loved the technique and used it all the time instead of marking a design or stitching in the ditch. Continuous curves are easy, but they give an awesome result.

The longer the arc, the more difficult it becomes to quilt. For learning, try curves that are one-and-a-half to three inches long.

QUILT A PRACTICE SAMPLE

This is a free-motion technique, so you will not be using feed dogs. Many of the curves in the sample will be quilted away from you, backward, so use a free-motion foot with good visibility. The foot can make or break this technique.

1. To learn the technique, use a ruler and a blue wash-out marker to draw an eight-inch square on a 12-inch muslin square. Inside the eight-inch square, draw a two-inch grid of vertical and horizontal lines. These lines are only guides, you will not be stitching on them, but you will be making your curved lines around them. Layer the muslin square with batting and backing squares.

2. With safety pins, pin baste your practice sandwich around the outside of the square and in between the vertical lines. The vertical lines will be quilted first, and the pins then removed, so don't worry if they cross some of the horizontal lines (Fig. 1–52).

Keep the pins straight so they don't get in the way as you quilt. Anything that causes you to stop in the middle of a curve will be a problem, so plan ahead.

3. Stitch the outside border of the drawn square, starting at the top-left corner. When you get back to this point, quilt a curve over to the first vertical line (Fig. 1–53).

4. Starting at the top of the first vertical line, quilt a curve toward yourself down the line. As you sew, be sure to look at the first grid intersection and make a gentle curve to that point.

It may help to use your wash-out blue marker to place a dot at the midpoint of each curve to use as a guide.

5. Pause at the point, then stitch the next curve on the opposite side of the line, making an "S" shape. Continue in this manner to the end of the first line (Fig. 1–54, page 80).

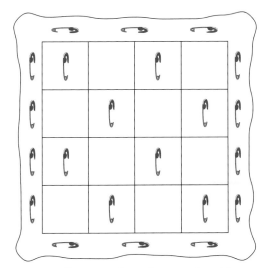

Fig. 1–52. Layer and pin the sample grid.

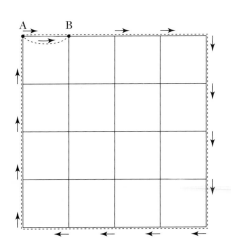

Fig. 1–53. Quilt the eight-inch square, starting and ending at A. Pause, then sew the first curve from A to B.

6. Stop, then quilt back up the line, quilting opposite the curves you have already quilted (Fig. 1–55).

7. At the top, quilt a curve over to the next vertical line, and quilt it in the same manner as the first line (Fig. 1–56). Work in this manner until all the vertical lines have been quilted.

8. At the top-right corner, quilt a curve down to the first horizontal line. Quilt that

line the same way you did the vertical lines (Fig. 1–57). Continue down the right side of the quilt, connecting the lines with a curve.

9. When all the horizontal lines have been quilted, quilt arcs to the left along the bottom edge and then up to the top-left corner so the entire square is covered with curves (Fig. 1–58).

When the marks are removed, you will have a beautiful background-fill design. If

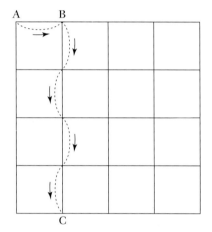

Fig. 1–54. Sew from B to C in "S" shapes.

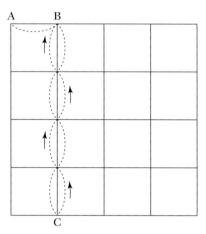

Fig. 1–55. Quilt backward from C to B.

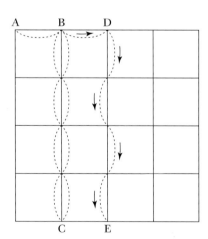

Fig. 1–56. Quilt from B to D, then from D to E.

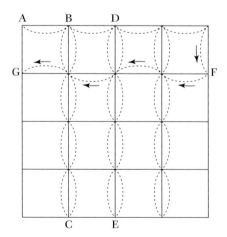

Fig. 1–57. Quilt from the top-right corner to F and continue to G.

this were pieced work, such as a nine-patch or Variable Star block, you would use the seam lines in place of the drawn grid (Fig. 1–59).

Quilt another line one-fourth inch from the outside edge, bind the square, and make yourself a lovely potholder. You can try out some of your machine embroidery stitches to add to the center of each curved "square."

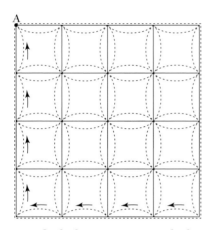

Fig. 1–58. Quilt the curves across the bottom and up the left side of the square to point A to complete the design.

APPLICATIONS

Continuous curves can be used to outline any piecing. They are especially useful for applications like stars, diamonds, Grandmother's Flower Garden hexagons, sawtooth borders, and nine-patches. Whenever I am stumped by a design, the first thing I will try is continuous curves.

If quilting an "S" shape is difficult for you, do the curves on one side of the line (or seam) first and then the other. Some quilters find this much easier than winding back and forth.

The order of quilting is important. Take the time to study the area to be quilted and plan a route for the curves so stopping and starting are kept to a minimum. Sometimes an area you are quilting with continuous curves may adjoin a block that needs a quilted motif. Rather than do the block separately later, you can take a side trip to do the block, then connect back to the continuous curves. After you have done several blocks or designs, you will have the route worked out and will be able to do as much as possible without reaching a dead end.

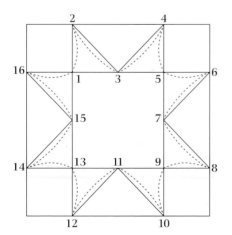

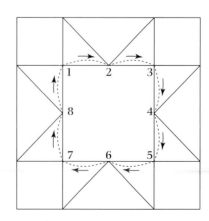

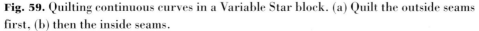

Fig. 59. Quilting continuous curves in a Variable Star block. (a) Quilt the outside seams first, (b) then the inside seams.

Feather Designs

FEEDING THE BIRDS

It is early in the morning after a big snow-fall, and you are still in your flannel nightgown, robe, and slippers, while having that hot coffee and breakfast. The cardinals, juncos, and chickadees line up near the empty bird feeder and give you hungry looks, making it impossible for you to enjoy your breakfast. So, you take pity on them, grab the bird seed, and plunge out the door, dressed just as you are. The snow is a foot deep and you hurry to the bird feeder and fill it as snow covers your flimsy slippers and soaks over the top. Job done, what next? Do you turn around and forge another trail through the snow and walk fast back to the warm kitchen? No! You back up slowly, placing your feet directly in the footprints already made on your trip out, and very carefully walk backward to the house, then hurry inside. Fast trip out, careful slow trip back.

What in the world does this have to do with quilting feathers?

The most important thing to remember about this story is the speed you use when feeding the birds – fast and smooth as you zip out to the feeder, then much slower as you re-trace your footsteps backward in the snow. This is probably the most important part of quilting feathers. Fast on the first pass over the shape, and then slower as you re-trace part of the path to get to the next feather.

TIPS FOR FEATHERS

When you machine quilt a feather design, the first thing to stitch is the spine. It's the central line of the design. If the design is a feathered wreath, the spine will be a circle. In a long border design, it is a center line.

SWEETHEART ON PARADE, 85" x 85". Based on vintage Amish and Mennonite sawtooth diamond designs, this classic is quilted with nylon monofilament thread. It was promised as a pledge to my cat Hillary if she would recover from a serious illness, and dedicated to her sweet nature. (Winner of the 1998 Bernina Award for Machine Workmanship and in the MAQS permanent collection.)

Likes most cats Hillary loves quilts and quilt fabrics.

Pin baste parallel to this line through the feathers to stabilize the piece for machine quilting (Fig. 1–60). Many times, this line will cover large areas of the quilt, and it will provide the anchor for the entire space you will be quilting, so the pinning here is crucial.

Place the pins with enough clearance for the free-motion foot so the pins need not be moved during the quilting of the spine and so they don't snag on the foot. Just when you think you will get by a pin, it will snag, causing a big glitch in the stitching line.

Don't play "chicken" with pins! With experience, you will know just how far out from the line to place the pins for the foot to clear them easily... yet they need to be close enough to the line to hold it securely.

Use your hands as a hoop to keep the quilting area smooth and taut so that the vital stabilizing line will go in flawlessly. All the rest of the quilting is based on this line. After the spine has been stitched, remove the pins that have been placed through the feather lines. Leave the pins that are outside the outer edges of the feather design in place to keep the entire design stable.

Quilt the feathers by starting on the inside of the design on the spine, quilt the first feather up and back down to the spine. As you approach the spine, slow down a bit so you don't go too far and overshoot the stopping point. Then take one or two stitches in place and proceed back over the line just stitched, going slower, looking ahead, and staying in control. This is called backtracking or double stitching. When you get back to the top of the next feather, you can speed up and quilt it right down to the spine (Fig. 1–61). Because of the repetition of stitching the feathers and because the double stitching is done on a line just quilted, your brain learns the action, and it becomes very comfortable for you.

I find that the double-stitched portion of a feather is easier to do in a vertical position or even at an angle rather than in a horizontal position.

The marks for feathers are simply guides to help you quilt them. If you veer off and one feather isn't quite the same as the next, it doesn't matter. They look prettier when

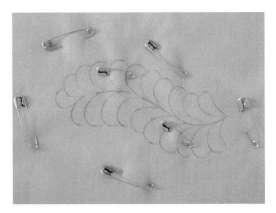

Fig. 1–60. Pin-basted feathers.

Fig. 1–61. You can hardly see the double stitching in a carefully quilted feather.

they are different sizes and heights. The smaller the angle as the feather meets the spine, the more graceful the final design will look. If the stencil you use is clunky looking, re-draw this part of each feather so it looks smooth and graceful. As you become more experienced at quilting feathers, you will be able to skip this re-drawing step and quilt the feathers more gracefully than they were drawn or traced (Fig. 1–62).

QUILTING OPTIONS

For quilting designs that are not continuous-line, like traditional feathers, it is important to plan ahead. The background quilting around the feather will determine how you quilt the feather design. For example, you can use the tops of the feathers as pathways to get from one line of the grid to the next. When quilting these feathers, you will want to double stitch their sides (Fig. 1–63).

For certain types of feathers, like very long skinny ones or long curved ones that are closely spaced, its better to double stitch a different part of the feather. It helps to have a double line for the spine for this method, because part of the spine will be used as a pathway for the double stitching. The other pathway will be the top portion of every other feather.

With this technique, the spine is quilted first, and if it's a double-line spine, quilt both lines first. Then proceed from the spine up the first feather and over its top. Continue over the top of the adjoining feather, then back down to the spine. Instead of re-tracing back up to the next feather, stitch along the spine, slowly and carefully, to the next feather.

Quilt up the side of the next feather, quickly and smoothly, and when you reach the top of the curve, stitch back to the pre-

vious feather to connect it, then double stitch back and proceed to the next feather top and then down (Fig. 1–64). This way, the short tops of the feathers and short portions of the spines are double stitched, rather than the more difficult long edges.

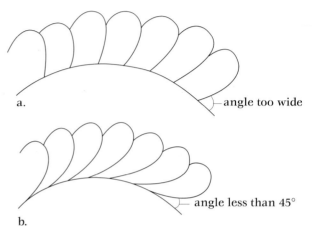

a. — angle too wide

b. — angle less than 45°

Fig. 1–62. (a) Clunky feathers. (b) Graceful feathers.

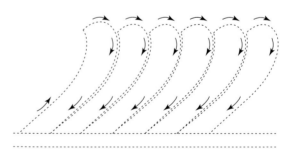

Fig. 1–63. Double stitching feathers along their sides.

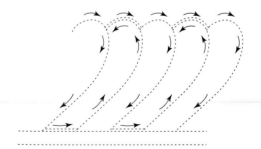

Fig. 1–64. Double stitch long feathers at the top and bottom.

When quilting feathers, you can switch back and forth between techniques as needed. You don't need to choose one method and stick with it for the entire design. Sometimes it will seem more comfortable and easier to do it one way and sometimes another, depending on the size, placement, and angle of each feather.

The smaller the feather, the easier it is to quilt. With small feathers, the quilt is moved just a little bit, so re-positioning the hands is minimal. The short, curvy lines are easy to sustain and keep even.

Feathers are easier to quilt if you use fine thread, a fine needle, and a short stitch length.

Lines and Grids

FREE-MOTION PARALLEL LINES

Many times, for background quilting, I like to do something that accurately replicates antique hand quilting (see SIXTEEN BASKETS OF MUD, page 126, and ORPHANED FEATHERED STAR, pages 112–113). For example, quilting straight lines about one-fourth inch apart, on the bias, makes a great antique-looking background (Fig. 1–65).

PARALLEL LINES HAVE SEVERAL ADVANTAGES:

• **They are not marked**, except for an occasional guide line to keep the lines parallel.

• **They can be done free motion**, so you don't have to stop and start every row.

• **Because the lines** are only one-fourth inch apart, double stitching over a previously stitched design or in the ditch is easy to do.

Quilt straight background lines on the bias so you don't stretch the quilt top. This appears to be reverse logic because we have been taught that bias stretches, but the bias accommodates straight-line quilting. The quilt doesn't stretch or distort, and no excess fabric is pushed along to the end of the line where it will become a pleat. If you did parallel lines or grids on the fabric grain, all of these problems would occur.

To keep free-motion parallel lines straight, use a ruler to mark a guide line in or near the center of the area to be quilted. I draw a new guide line every few inches. You can also use seams, borders, or parts of a quilting design as guide lines.

The first line quilted should be in the center of an area to stabilize it. Pin baste on each side of the marked line and remove the pins when this line has been stitched.

Any time you plan to double stitch or do close work (lines one-fourth to one-half inch apart), it is a good idea to use a small needle, #70 or #60 sharp, and fine thread so the thread build-up doesn't show.

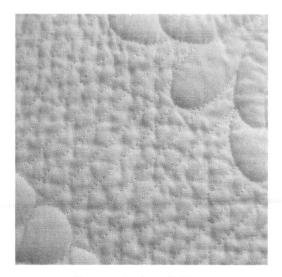

Fig. 1–65. Free-motion parallel lines.

Be sure you use a free-motion foot for parallel lines and grids because this foot will "float" above the quilt's surface without pushing or pulling the fabric. You should not have to pull on a quilt to get it to move under the foot. It should slide smoothly by moving only your fingertips. If the clearance of the foot isn't high enough for the quilt to move effortlessly under it, you won't be able to do this type of quilting.

As you quilt each parallel line, be sure to look at the line you just stitched, not at the needle. Some quilters look at the edge of the free-motion foot and use that as a guide. Look ahead of the needle and aim at a point. The line will be much straighter than if you look at the line as it is being quilted. If you find your lines are veering off and not staying parallel, don't try to correct the problem all at once with the very next line. Do it slowly over two or three lines so it won't be obvious.

Shorter lines are easier to quilt than very long lines. In a short line, the quilt doesn't have to be moved as far and as often, stopping and starting within the line are minimized, and control is easier and better.

Fig. 1–66. Cross-hatched grid quilting.

CROSS-HATCHED GRIDS

"Do I have to stop and start every single line in this grid?" asked my student, holding out an eight-inch feathered wreath design with a one-half-inch grid in the center. She was appalled that it would take forever to start and stop each line of stitches, and she felt it could be done better and faster with hand quilting.

Free-motion quilting is the answer, and it works wonderfully in cross-hatched grids. A little planning is necessary, but the quilting goes quickly. It is good experience in control and speed, and it makes a beautiful result that adds much to the complexity of the quilting.

If you think the design you are quilting would be faster by hand, then you know you are doing something wrong. Unless a grid covers the entire surface or the major central portion of a quilt, it can be done free motion with the "ricochet" technique. Just as a pool ball bounces from one side of the table to the other, grid lines can be sewn in the same way. Whenever you come to the end of a stitching line, continue as if you had hit the edge of the design and bounced to the next line. These changes of direction are usually at a 90-degree angle (Fig. 1–66).

If a line stops at an end point with no other line near it, there are two choices: end the line and start another line at a different point, or double stitch over a line of quilting to get to the starting point of a new line.

The ricochet technique involves considerable variation in speed with the foot control. The speed needs to be fairly fast on the line, but as you approach the end point, it is necessary to slow the motor speed and your hands so they are synchronized to keep the stitches even. Slow down even more as you reach the end point, then pivot and resume speed on the next line. Use an even slower speed if you have to double stitch.

It is a common misconception that one constant speed is the desired goal for machine quilting. Vary the speed to suit the task. Stippling needs a fast, constant rate, whereas grids require a variety of speeds, so the end points are sharp, the lines are straight and even, and the double stitching is unnoticeable.

When you are dead-ended and can find no nearby line to quilt, stop, lock in the line of stitching, and cut the threads. Resume quilting in another area. There may be two or three stops in an entire grid with the ricochet technique, which is far better than stopping at every single line if you use a walking foot.

Check the completed grid carefully and look for any "orphans," lines that have not been quilted. Sometimes they are more obvious if you turn the quilt over and look at the back.

One of my prize-winning quilts had been in at least four judged shows. When I had the quilt at a lecture, someone pointed out to me that a grid line was missing. I was amazed that I had never noticed it and that the judges hadn't either. Yes, I did go back and quilt the missing line!

Stippling

My students are all assembled, sitting at their machines, and they are excited and ready to stipple. They are amazed when, instead of starting with their sewing machines, I ask them to get out a pencil as I pass out sheets of drawing paper. Before they can stitch the stipple shapes, they need to have an idea of what the shapes look like, how to draw them, how to build them, and how to echo them to form areas of machine stippling that are evenly spaced and sized, with no points. Drawing stippling really helps to lock the technique in your brain before you go to the sewing machine. Too many students founder at the machine because they have no idea what to quilt, where to quilt, or how to make shapes.

What is stippling? Everyone loves the look of this wonderful machine-quilting technique. It comes in all sorts of sizes and shapes, and it is as personal as handwriting. Stippling is used to fill space with even, closely spaced, parallel curvy lines. It is a term also used in other media, such as painting or woodworking. Both stippling and meandering have the same shaped elements that are built up and repeated, but stippling is much smaller in scale (Fig. 1–67). Anything spaced under one-fourth inch apart is termed stippling.

Fig. 1–67. (a) Meander quilting. (b) Stippling.

Although I am now adept at stippling, several years ago I absolutely refused to use it. Then, while washing my blue and white Spode dishes one day, I realized that my plates had stippling shapes used as background-fill in the rose design. The pattern, called "Primula," was first introduced in 1898 (Fig. 1–68). Suddenly, I looked at stippling in a whole new light. It would work wonderfully on my traditional quilts to reproduce museum-quality stippling fast. I hadn't tried to stipple in more than five years, but it was time to analyze this stitch and learn how to do it.

I tried tackling the elusive stipple stitch one more time, with much more success. My new sewing machine helped tremendously. The new machines have incredible controls so that you can easily adjust your speed to the level of your expertise.

My biggest mistake had been to listen to varied advice from people who all agreed on one thing: Pedal to the metal! Floor it! Make the table shake!

After experimenting, I found that, for a beginner like me, a medium speed was best. It was fast enough to insure progress and create smooth shapes but slow enough so I didn't end up a wreck with out-of-control stitching.

As a rule of thumb, the bigger the size of the stippling or meandering shape, the faster the machine should go. When you do tiny shapes for a background design, a medium speed is best, so you don't end up with crazy, erratic stitching.

After a little effort and analysis, I found that, not only was I successful at stippling, but I was enjoying it and planning to use it to set off designs and trapunto and to create surface texture. I can stipple and breathe simultaneously! I can stipple and talk! Sometimes, after stippling for many minutes, I do not even remember how I got to that place in the quilt. It has become automatic, like driving home the same route every day.

The following sections present some of the things I learned teaching myself to stipple, starting with the design of the free-motion foot and including a detailed description of how to make stippling shapes and control the fabric.

FREE-MOTION FOOT

For your machine, you will need a darning foot or free-motion quilting foot

Fig. 1–68. Stippling on a Spode plate.

that has enough clearance when the feed dogs are dropped or covered to allow the quilt to move with no resistance, like you are ice skating, not slogging through sand.

I adjust my machine so the presser foot sits quite high, loses its "bounce," and skims over the surface of the quilt. I do all my stippling with this setting, but for other types of quilting, I set the foot a little lower so the bounce returns and each stitch can be felt as the foot bounces along.

The foot you choose is a vital but comparatively inexpensive ingredient in stippling, yet many quilters use the one that came with the machine or the one the salesperson said was "good for free-motion quilting." It is up to you to investigate, buy a different foot, see what the company offers in addition to what the store stocks, or modify one you already have so that you have the best possible tool to do stippling.

THE DESIGN OF THE FOOT IS IMPORTANT. LOOK FOR THE FOLLOWING FEATURES:

• **It is crucial that you have good visibility.** You can't space lines of stippling if you can't see the line you have just stitched. If the front of the foot you are using covers the line you are trying to see, it is doing more harm than good.

• **Look for a free-motion foot** that has an open toe. If you have a foot that does not have an open toe, you can cut out the front of the foot for greater visibility.

• **For a few brands of machines,** you can get a foot with an offset shank that allows visibility to the back, so you can see where you are going (Fig. 1–69). This foot can be used for all free-motion quilting, especially when following a line.

• **A larger foot is helpful** if you can't find one with an open toe. The larger foot has quite a large area of clear visibility, so you can see to space the stippling. Sometimes they have a higher clearance too.

• **There are many options available** for stippling feet. Some are so difficult to work with though that, no matter how hard I try, I cannot do acceptable stippling with them. Clear plastic feet tend to distort what you are seeing and may even prevent you from seeing the stitches.

My own machine has various choices. Several are excellent, and some don't work for me at all. Experiment and try several feet at the store before you decide which will work the best.

Fig. 1–69. Use a free-motion foot with an offset shank for greater visibility.

NEEDLE AND THREAD

Needles and thread make a big difference. The standard #70 needle and #50 cotton thread are fine for larger shapes, but if you decide to try small shapes for stippling, a smaller needle like a #60 sharp combined with a #60 two-ply cotton thread, #100 silk thread, or nylon monofilament thread works best. The needle holes will be as small as possible, preventing the work from looking like a mass of unconnected puncture wounds. The holes will still be there, and you will be able to see through them if you hold the quilt up to light, but they will be almost undetectable.

Small needle holes help eliminate bobbin pop-ups, in which the bobbin thread comes through on the top. Tension on the top thread can be adjusted to accommodate the different pressures stippling puts on stitch formation.

STIPPLING SHAPES

The shapes look like pieces from a jigsaw puzzle or pieces of coral, little mittens, reindeer antlers, or even Mickey Mouse ears. Stippling lines do not cross each other – no intersections on these little roads!

Keep in mind that, when you are trying to create stippling shapes, they are formed when curvy lines wind around and parallel each other. It isn't one shape repeated over and over. It is the interlocking of curves with shapes on the curves themselves that creates stippling. Don't try to copy the shapes that someone else quilts. Your stippling will be like your handwriting, very individual. Some stippling looks like bubbles or circles, and some has shapes that are long and skinny. As long as these shapes are evenly spaced and interlock to give a wonderful texture that flattens down the quilt, they are fine.

My stippling has changed from large and bubbly when I started to much more long and wormy looking. I looked at many examples of hand stippling to get my inspiration and then adapted that look to what I was comfortable with in machine quilting.

Stippling shapes tend to mirror the presser foot shape. If the foot is round, your shapes will tend to be round; oblong foot, oblong shapes. The brain sees the presser foot and subconsciously mirrors it. A larger foot can cause you to make larger shapes. When I recently switched to a much smaller foot with an opening in the front, my stippling became smaller and more precise immediately.

STITCH LENGTH

The stitch length for stippling is necessarily shorter than for other types of machine quilting because the machine's speed needs to be faster. Smaller stitches also allow smooth curves in the small shapes. Points on these curvy shapes are caused by moving your hand too fast or "scrubbing floors" with your hands.

Slow your hands way down and speed up the machine – slow hands, fast foot.

The sound of the sewing machine as you run it fast might be a problem for you. Many quilters hear that sound and can't help but speed up their hands to keep up with it. Also, the sound makes some quilters nervous and tense. Sometimes playing music helps because it covers up the machine noise. However, you could find yourself quilting to the beat of the music, which may cause jerky movements. Perhaps audio books or a TV show with a lot of dialog will help mask the sound of the sewing machine. Once you learn the combination of slow hands, fast foot, you will be able to stipple without thinking.

STIPPLING SIZE

The size of the stippling depends on your project. An entire background area of a quilt would call for meandering. The center of a five-inch feathered wreath would require the much smaller stippling. You can do different sizes of stippling on the same project.

Stippling shapes should be smaller than the smallest element of the design you are surrounding. For example, the stippling shape should be smaller than the smallest feather in a feather wreath.

CONTROL

When you first learn to stipple, you may go slow and your shapes may be small and cramped, or you may feel wild and out of control, then settle down. After you quilt for five to ten minutes, you will warm up, and your sewing will level out to the correct combination of motor speed and hand movement. As you quilt for longer periods of time, your machine's speed will increase without your even being aware of it.

You will find that you have to keep the size of the shapes even throughout the quilt so you don't start with teeny shapes and end up with huge loosely spaced ones or vice versa. It is important to keep the spacing between the lines even as well. Every time you sit down to stipple, you may want to practice on a sample piece for a few minutes before you tackle your quilt.

STARTING THE DESIGN

I usually start stitching right at the quilting design to be surrounded with stippling (Fig. 1–70). I then work away from the design, out to a seam line, the edge of the quilt, or over to the edge of another design. It's best not to begin out in the middle of an open space.

To cross a space to get to another area, it's best to meander, in an arc, over to the next design edge, rather than sew straight toward it (Fig. 1–71). I also stipple right up to and touch the stitching on quilted

Fig. 1–70. Begin stippling on the edge of an already quilted design.

Fig. 1–71. Crossing a space with meandering.

designs. This really makes them stand out and doesn't create a "no-man's land" of space between the design and the stippling.

BUILDING STIPPLING

Building stippling is like building a brick wall. Start at the bottom and build up and away from yourself. That way you will be able to space the stippling by looking at the line you have already quilted. Because the previous line is in front of the foot, the shapes will unfold right in front of you, and the spacing will be easier to control. When you realize you are sewing off into blank space, you will relax, and when you relax, the quilting will improve dramatically.

The great fear is crossing over a previous line of stitching because it can be difficult to see what you are doing while working at speed. This is especially true if you are using nylon invisible thread. Working away from yourself eliminates this problem.

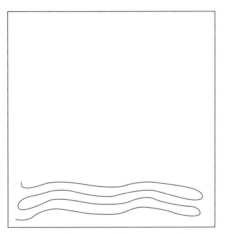

Fig. 1–72. Start with horizontal wavy lines of echo quilting.

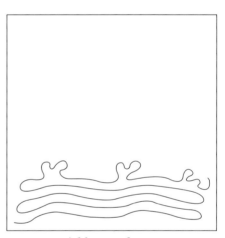

Fig. 1–73. Add some shapes.

Fig. 1–74. Echo quilt the added shapes.

Fig. 1–75. Continue echo quilting and adding shapes.

INCLUDE ECHO QUILTING

Much of the design consists of small units of stippling connected with echo quilting. It is not always necessary to be drawing shapes. Echo quilting gives you resting time when you don't have to think about what you are doing, what shapes to draw, or where to go. You simply parallel the shapes and lines you have already quilted. It is like coasting downhill on a bicycle.

PRACTICE DRAWING

Practice by drawing before trying stippling on the sewing machine. Don't worry if your shapes don't look like the illustrations. Stippling is as unique as handwriting.

- **Begin with some horizontal wavy lines** of echo quilting (Fig. 1–72). Do as many as it takes to get comfortable.

- **Add some mitten shapes** to the next line of echo quilting, or perhaps some Mickey Mouse ears as you go along, spacing them as you echo (Fig. 1–73).

- **Echo the shapes** as you return to the edge of your piece (Fig. 1–74)

- **For the next line,** continue echoing and at the same time add more shapes (Fig. 1–75).

- **Keep echoing the line** you just stitched, adding more shapes, then echoing the shapes. Try not to go back and forth. Instead, change direction for a while and then echo downward to continue the design.

Most of my stippling ends up looking like a mountain with the slope going up to the right. I then echo down the mountain, back to the foothills, and start building shapes and echoing them over and over until another area has been filled (Fig. 1–76).

WORKING-IN EXCESS FABRIC

Many times, a bubble of fabric will appear between quilted areas. The only technique I've found that works well to flatten and evenly disperse the extra fabric is stippling. Other techniques like echo quilting or crosshatched grid quilting may only make the problem worse, creating further stretching and distortion and resulting in pleats and tucks.

The basic strategy for working in a bubble is to surround and conquer it. Instead of stippling straight across an area, form a basin or bowl shape and quilt side to side or surround the area with a circle and work toward the middle. You can gradually work in the extra fabric, and it won't be noticeable in the "puckers" of the stippling (Fig. 1–77, page 96).

An aid like an awl, or even your fingertip, helps to manipulate the excess fabric and work it under the needle. Be careful to keep your finger away from the needle! You can tweak the excess fabric and work it

Fig. 1–76. Build a unit of shapes.

into the stippling so it doesn't show. However, sometimes it is all but impossible, and a few little odds and ends of fabric might get sewn down in the stippling. They will blend in with the overall result, and the shrinkage of the cotton batt, when the quilt is washed, will help camouflage a problem area to some extent.

Some fabrics will "stipple in" more easily than others. Heavy, stiff fabrics tend to make pleats, as do finely woven fabrics. The easiest to work with are the looser woven, muslin-type soft cottons. Be sure to audition any fabric that will be used for extensive background stippling before you commit to it in a quilt. Sometimes another fabric in the same color will work much better and give a better result because of its feel ("hand") and the way it shrinks and allows the stippling to give it texture.

The basic strategy for working in a bubble is to surround and conquer.

HARD-TO-REACH AREAS

What do you do about those little nooks and crannies, those hard-to-reach areas? Go into them by bumping along the edge of one side, much like a ball bounces, until you get into the area as far as possible (Fig. 1–78). Make a squiggly, wormy line to sneak your way out again. Then continue stippling as before.

It's important to slow down, to gain control, and watch where you are going

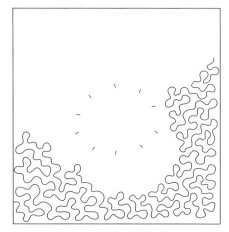

Fig. 1–77. Surround a bubble of excess fabric with stippling. Work in the fabric as you stipple toward the center of the bubble.

Fig. 1–78. Bounce into narrow areas, then stipple your way out.

Fig. 1–79. Double stitch to get out of a tight spot.

when you are working in tight places like these. Sometimes it's easiest to stipple all the way into a nook or cranny, knowing that you will stop at the end. Cut the thread, take a break, and resume quilting in another area.

You can also get out of a tight spot by backtracking over a line of a quilting design. Much like quilting a feather, use the stitched line as a pathway to double back and get to a clear area for more stippling. I would use this technique only if the distance was fairly short, less than an inch or so (Fig. 1–79).

RELAXING

One student asked me why she had such terribly chapped lips after she had stippled a big quilt. We all laughed and told her she was sticking out her tongue in concentration, and the constant moisture had chapped her lips. It's difficult to relax when you are stippling. Even now, I find the first day or two of stippling on a large quilt gives me sore muscles, but then I get into the rhythm and relax, and all is well.

Relaxing is key to doing good stippling. Learn to get into a rhythm and enjoy the process. Don't look at all there is to stipple, but concentrate instead on the area you are doing. To relax, try to concentrate on each muscle and get it to relax and then try some more quilting. Vary your set-up if you are getting sore and stiff. Try some yoga. Play some music.

For the foot control, use the same foot as your dominant hand – right-handed, right foot; left-handed, left foot. If you have a knee lever and it is in the way, take it out. You don't need it for stippling. Put your other foot up on something that is the same height as the foot on the control so

your back is more comfortable. Having your feet at different levels can sometimes cause lower-back pain.

TIPS FOR STIPPLING

1. Practice some wavy lines first to get the feel before you try stippling. Start making them smaller and more closely spaced. Then try the puzzle shapes and join them together with curvy lines.

2. Limit your sessions to 15 to 20 minutes and take breaks by doing something physical, like sweeping the floor or taking a brisk walk.

3. Even stippling is more important than tiny stippling, just as in hand quilting.

4. Divide large shapes. If one of the shapes is too large compared to the others, it will look like a "pimple" on your quilt. Go back and divide it up with another line of stitching.

5. Don't forget to blink! Especially if you wear contact lenses, look up every few minutes, blink, focus on something far away, or close your eyes completely to let the muscles you use for focusing relax and re-charge. You will be able to stipple better and for longer periods if you take these rest breaks for your eyes.

FREQUENT FREE-MOTION QUESTIONS

Q: Why are my stippling shapes pointed?

A: The most common cause of sharp points on stippling is moving your hands way too fast. Slow them down. Keep your hand speed calm and even, and run the machine at a medium speed. It may be that the sound of the machine is causing you to speed up your hands. Find the combination of machine and hand speeds that works best for you and that produces the best looking stitches. You also need to know that, to avoid points and corners, your stippling stitches need to be shorter than your regular quilting stitches.

Q: What happens if I run out of bobbin thread right in the middle of a design?

A: Clip any loose threads, and after you re-wind the bobbin and begin quilting again, insert the needle for the first stitch back about one-fourth inch into the line of stitching rather than at the very spot where you left off. Take the usual small stitches right over the previous stitches and then continue quilting normally. If you are careful, this break in the stitching will be secure without being noticeable.

Q: Does a hoop for machine quilting help with free-motion?

A: For some people, the hoop gives them the feeling that they are "driving" and that everything is being held firm, so no pleats are formed. This confidence allows them to learn to quilt. I think of the hoops for machine quilting as quilters' training wheels – something you could try for learning how to quilt or to aid you if you have physical problems, like arthritis. I find it easier to quilt without a hoop, because that's the way I learned, and I believe that a hoop just gets in the way. If you think it might help, give it a try.

Q: Once I begin quilting a continuous-line design, I get lost. Help!

A: A continuous-line design is drawn as one long line, much like a piece of spaghetti, all twirled and looped on itself. When you quilt such a design, you will sometimes be quilting backward, and it can be difficult to tell where to go next. It's easy to go off in the wrong direction. I recommend that you study the design first, trace it with your finger, and mentally plan a route. If you get confused when quilting, stop the machine and look at the design to figure out where to go next. The time saved by not having to un-sew a mistake is well worth taking your time.

Some students have the misconception that once you begin to quilt a design, you must not stop at all, ever. Nonsense! Stop any time you need to adjust your hands, see where you are going, answer the phone, go to the bathroom. But be careful when you resume that you first put the needle up and then begin slowly so you don't have a very obvious wobble where you start up the quilting line again.

Q: Why should I look ahead of the needle when following a marked design in free-motion quilting?

A: Looking ahead of the needle gives you something to aim at. If your brain knows where you are going from signals from your eyes, your movements become synchronized, smooth, and even. It is like driving a car. You don't look at the road as it disappears under the front of the car; instead, you focus ahead, watching where you are going.

Q: What stitch length is good for machine quilting?

A: This is a personal decision. You can use the standard length of about 12 stitches per inch, or you can make the stitches larger or smaller, depending on personal preference. I have seen beautiful machine quilting done both ways. Many times it depends on the style of quilting. Folk-art quilts might look nicer with a heavier thread and a longer stitch than heirloom quilts with their tiny feathers and stippling. On heirlooms, I use a very fine thread and a much shorter stitch length. Stippling requires the shortest stitch of all so the shapes have nice rounded forms without corners and spikes. Machine quilting isn't like hand quilting – smaller doesn't mean better. However, consistency is very important. The stitches should be the same length throughout the quilt.

Q: Do the lines in echo quilting have to be evenly spaced?

A: It is up to you whether you try to space them evenly for a more traditional look or vary the spacing, giving it a more modern grass-cloth-like texture. Make a practice piece and see what you like best. If you try for evenly spaced lines, there is still some latitude. The lines do not have to be perfectly spaced as in a grid.

A VISIT TO WALES, 23" x 23". This miniature whole-cloth quilt contains original designs based loosely on Welsh quilts and motifs. A detail is shown on page 86. (Quilter's Dream® batt, silk thread.)

QUILTING SAMPLES

Perhaps I am overly cautious, but I have found that it is invaluable in preventing problems down the road to take the time to quilt a sample before going ahead with an entire quilt top. With a sample, you can check the backing fabric, marking tools, quilting design, thread, and batting, and the sample can then be used as a reference.

BACKGROUND FABRIC

Many times, I make a small sample sandwich of the background fabric, batting, and backing and quilt it with the most densely quilted designs to be used in the quilt. I do this before I make the quilt top, just to be sure the background fabric quilts well and washes up nicely. There have been occasions when the background fabric did not quilt well because it was too stiff or too stretchy. So I decided against using it in the quilt, even though I had already purchased the full amount. It wouldn't be worth it! Better to check the fabric at this point than to spoil a beautiful quilt top.

MARKING TOOLS

By using a small piece of the background fabric in the sample and marking it with various choices, you will see right away which markers can be seen and removed easily. You may reconsider a fabric if you have to use a white pencil to see the quilting designs.

QUILTING DESIGN

Sometimes the best design on paper is a nightmare to quilt. Making a sample with the quilting design you want to mark on the quilt will tell you many things. First, do you enjoy quilting it? I have loved some of the designs I have drawn, only to find they were almost impossibly difficult to quilt. A simple change at this point will prevent hours of frustration in trying to quilt something that is out of your skill level or that you don't like doing. Second, it isn't easy to see what a design will look like from a line drawing or a stencil, and quilting it on a sample of an actual fabric to be used in the quilt will reveal a lot.

After quilting the sample, pin the quilt top to your design wall, then pin the quilted sample to the corresponding area on the quilt. Stand back and take a good long look. Designs appear totally different when viewed from several feet away rather than from a few inches away, and seeing them in the context of the quilt makes a difference, too. I have switched design choices many times at this point. The design may have looked fine on paper, but after the sample was quilted and pinned to the real thing, I could see right away it wasn't right for the quilt.

Try several samples and live with them for awhile before you decide which designs you like. Quilting a sample will also tell you how much time is involved in finishing each motif and whether or not you want to devote that much time to a particular project. As you become more experienced and try different designs, you will know many of these things without having to quilt each one.

THREADS AND NEEDLES

Make a sample by using the threads and needles you are considering for the actual quilt. Don't use any old thing that is in the machine. With a sample, you can adjust the tension and play with the thread choices in the needle and bobbin to get the best possible look. If you are debating between different threads, use them all in the sample and label them so you can compare how they look in the completed quilting. I have changed my mind here, too, because of the way the threads quilted up in my sample.

BATTING CHOICE

One of the most vital ingredients for how the quilting will look is the batting, and in the samples you make, you can narrow the selection and actually feel how the batting affects the quilting. Is it thin or thick enough? Does it shrink enough or too much when you wash the sample? Will it give the dimension the design needs?

Checking all the components before doing the actual quilt may seem like a huge chore, but it really requires only one or two small quilted samples because you can try many things out at the same time. These samples are terrific reference guides, and they make handy test areas for checking things like tension adjustment as you work on the real quilt.

As a bonus, in making a sample, you will teach yourself how to quilt a design before you do it for the first time on an actual quilt. You will be able to see all the pitfalls, learn what to change, and give your brain a "patterning" lesson, so it will be that much easier when you work on the quilt.

FINISHING TIPS

Squaring the Quilt

After you have completed the machine quilting but before you bind the quilt, there are a few things to do. First of all, dampen the entire quilt. The starch you used in piecing the quilt will keep the edges stable, so don't immerse the quilt, just spray it until it is wet. Flatten the quilt so it is square while it is wet. Allow it to air dry so it will shrink up and flatten out before binding.

When it is dry, if there are stubborn places on the edges, such as lumps and bumps and waves, run some short lines of machine basting stitches along the edge in those areas. Then ease in the excess fabric. Use strong thread that won't break when you pull on the top thread. This technique is similar to easing-in a sleeve cap in garment sewing.

Planning ahead will help make the squaring-up process easy. Cut the final border strips (if they are plain and not pieced) about an inch wider than needed. This extra width will provide trimming room for squaring the quilt.

To square the quilt, measure the distance through the center crosswise and lengthwise, then make sure the outside edges are these same measurements before you put on the binding. Many times, you will find that only the top and bottom have stretched a bit during quilting because they have been quilted on the cross grain, which stretches more easily than the lengthwise grain. In addition, you may find that the quilt's edges, which were perfectly straight before quilting, are now sticking out in some places, sometimes more than half an inch.

For a quilt with a plain border, the answer is to use a large square ruler and a fine-line permanent pen to mark a new edge for the quilt top, as follows: Measuring from the border seam, mark the width of the border plus the seam allowance in several places along the edge of the quilt. Connect the marks to make a straight line for the new edge. Be sure that the measurement from the last border seam is consistent all around the quilt and that the corners are square (Fig. 1–80).

Sometimes there will be no distortion in the quilt's edges, in which case, you can skip marking a new edge. If the final border is pieced, such as a sawtooth border, then this step is not applicable.

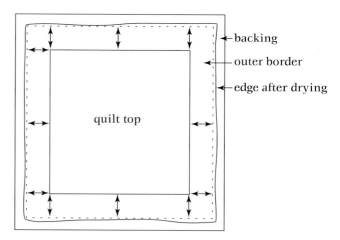

Fig. 1–80. Marking a new quilt edge after the quilt has been wetted and dried.

If pieced borders differ in length, machine baste along the edge and ease in the extra fabric. Easing will not be noticeable after the binding has been sewn on and the quilt has been washed because the batting shrinkage will camouflage it. Be careful not to ease in so much that you create gathers or pleats.

BINDING THE EDGES

The binding is the picture frame for the quilt. It finishes it and gives the design its final border or boundary, and getting rid of all that excess backing and batting makes it look so much better.

FOR ME THERE IS SIMPLY NO QUESTION ABOUT WHICH BINDING METHOD TO USE. USE BIAS!

• **It looks better.**

• **It stays smooth and rounded.**

• **It doesn't develop little lines** and crinkles in it after washing.

• **It acts like an elastic band** around the outside of the quilt to hold it in properly.

• **If bias binding is prepared correctly,** it works beautifully, and even a beginner can do it successfully.

• **It is just as easy** to use the rotary cutter and ruler to cut two-inch bias strips as it is to use them to cut two-inch straight strips.

• **Bias binding really improves the look** and stability of a quilt.

After the bias strips have been cut and the ends cut precisely at a 45-degree angle,

sew the ends together with a short stitch length. Press the seam allowances open.

Press the binding strip in half, wrong sides together. While pressing, stretch the strip gently and use spray starch to give it stability and crispness, much like purchased bias tape. Be sure you have made enough to go around the entire quilt and overlap a bit where the ends will join. I usually put the joined ends off center on the top edge of the quilt (Fig. 1–81).

Use your walking foot to apply the binding and don't trim off the excess batting or backing until the binding has been applied. Be sure you leave a one-fourth-inch seam allowance. It is sometimes difficult to judge, especially if the walking foot is larger than your regular sewing foot.

You don't need to pin the binding on, just align the backing's raw edges with the quilt top's raw edges. Then slowly and carefully sew on the binding, folding and mitering the corners as you go.

Trim off the excess batting and backing as well as a smidgen of the binding itself in the seam allowances on all sides of the quilt. With a narrow binding like I use (two-inch strips), trimming this closely will allow the binding to fold over to the back of

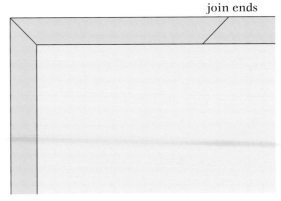

Fig. 1–81. Join the binding ends off center on the top edge of the quilt.

the quilt and still cover the stitching line. Trim carefully at the corners so the binding will fall into place easily and make a mitered corner.

Pin the binding as you fold it over to the back, easing it along with your thumb and fingers. I find that the long silk pins work great for this. Because they are sharp and long, they will easily penetrate the thicknesses of fabric, but they aren't so big that they get in your way when hand sewing.

Hand sew the back of the binding with tiny invisible stitches. A #60 embroidery thread in a neutral shade works for many colors, or you can match the color of your thread to the binding. If you have to sew through close stippling, you can get a very sore finger, so be sure to use a thimble. Check every now and then to make sure the stitches aren't showing through on the front of the quilt. Be sure to sew the miters closed at each corner.

Hand sewing the binding is one of the most enjoyable parts of making a quilt for me. With the quilt draped softly over my lap, I can see the beautiful stitches and designs on the back of the quilt as I work my way along the binding. It gives me a chance to examine the back of the quilt for loose threads so they can be clipped before the quilt is officially finished.

WASHING THE QUILT

It is time for the last step in getting the look of an heirloom for this machine-quilted quilt – washing it! Too many quilters cringe when I tell them that it is this final step that creates the magic in machine quilting. Washing the quilt does great things for the final look. Machine quilting tends to make a quilt stiff and flat, and washing it gently in modern laundry equipment will

soften it and cause the batting to shrink a bit, giving the quilting designs dimension and making that flat board-like look disappear. Just like washing new blue jeans to soften them and make them more usable, washing and tumbling break down the bonds in the quilt to make it supple. Washing also removes excess starch, marking chemicals, and water-soluble thread. It also removes the grime from months of working with the quilt.

Washing lets you block the quilt, shape it to size, square up corners, smooth out bumps, and mash down bulges. Cotton is a natural fiber, so just like hair, it can be stretched, smoothed, and manipulated when wet, then allowed to dry in the shape you placed it.

HERE ARE THE STEPS FOR WASHING YOUR FINISHED QUILT:

• Be sure the washer is clean, doesn't have residue from other laundry chemicals such as bleach, and is free of pet hair, etc.

• Load the quilt in the machine by starting at one corner and gently arranging the entire quilt, on the diagonal, around the agitator (Fig. 1–84).

• Fill the washer with cool water. While the washer is filling, gently press down on the quilt to make sure it is completely submerged (Fig. 1–85).

• Let the quilt soak, then use the spin cycle (select the gentle spin, if you have one) to remove the water.

• Re-fill the washer with lukewarm water and add a small amount of dissolved quilt soap. Use a hand wash or delicate cycle, and select the highest water level so there is plenty water to do the job.

One wash cycle is enough for a small wall quilt. However, I usually wash a large quilt about four times through the gentle cycle, using soap only in the first wash.

• If you like, you can add a small amount of liquid fabric softener to the final rinse, after the washer has filled with water so it will dilute properly and not stain the quilt.

• Use the spin cycle again to remove water (Fig. 1–86). The quilt is now ready to go into the dryer.

DRYING THE QUILT

Gently lift the quilt from the washer, supporting it from underneath with both hands. Bundle the quilt with the wrong side out so the right side won't rub on the dryer walls. I usually tumble it dry on very low heat for about five minutes, less for a small quilt. The dryer will get out the excess water left in from the low spin speed and will also soften the quilt a bit.

Fig. 1–84. Loading the washing machine. (a) Start with one corner. (b) Arrange the quilt loosely around the agitator.

Fig. 1–85. Press the quilt down in the water.

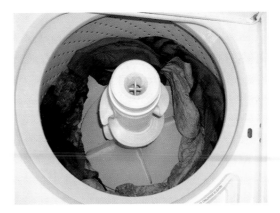

Fig. 1–86. After the final spin cycle, the quilt is ready to remove and dry.

Fig. 1–87. The author smooths and squares up a wet quilt. A plastic sheet protects the floor.

Prepare a place for air drying the quilt. This should be all set and ready for when the quilt comes out of the dryer, or the washer if you skip the dryer step. For a small quilt, you can use a cutting table, kitchen island counter, or any flat surface where the quilt can be undisturbed and get plenty of ventilation.

For large quilts, I clear a space on a floor, preferably in a room which can be closed off so pets or children don't disturb it. Large, yard trash bags, cut open and spread out on the floor, will protect the floor from the wet quilt, as would a plastic drop cloth or a vinyl tablecloth.

To block the quilt, carefully place the still very damp quilt on the floor or table and spread it out (Fig. 1–87). You can eyeball it as you work to make it square and straight. Remember, it will dry in the position you place it, so if the corners are off, they will dry that way. A quilt with a cotton batt is extremely malleable at this point and easy to either improve or distort. Gently push and pull it here and there until it is flat and square, the best you can get it. Pay special attention to the corners to create 90-degree angles.

Let the quilt air dry. Set up some fans; turn up the heat; turn up the air conditioning. Whatever the season or temperature, use some aids to shorten the drying time. It usually takes 24 hours for a big quilt to dry. For good measure, let it stay in place another day to make sure it is dry before handling it again. If you remove it while damp to work on or hang it, the quilt will stretch and become distorted. If you fold it while damp, it will crease. Whatever you do, don't hang it over a line or porch rail.

When the quilt is completely dry, place it on a work table and go over it to remove debris, like stray threads and pet hair. This is when I use a permanent ink pen to place a dot of color on any bobbin pop-ups that appear on the top. If you need a magnifying glass, be sure to use one.

MAKING A LABEL

While your quilt is drying is a good time to spend an hour or more to design and make a lovely label. You will want to include the quilt name, pattern name, your name, date, location, any special information, a dedication, or a verse. Don't put this

step off. If you say, "Oh, I'll do that later, I just want to get this thing up and hanging, or on the bed," chances are you won't ever do it. Even if it is a simple traced label or a piece of muslin with the information written on it in permanent ink, it will document the quilt. You can also use a computer ink-jet printer to print labels on freezer paper-backed muslin or special fabric made for this purpose. For me, this is one of the most enjoyable parts of the entire process. I will spend several hours happily playing with my set of colored pens, drawing and creating a simple but pretty label that will be the final touch for my quilt, as well as provide the necessary documentation.

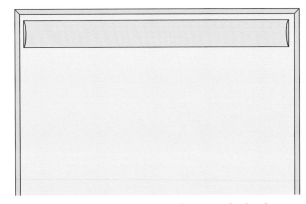

Fig. 1–88. Adding a hanging sleeve to the back.

ADDING A HANGING SLEEVE

If your quilt will ever be displayed, it will need a sleeve for hanging (Fig. 1–88). Use fabric from the backing of the quilt for the sleeve so it is unobtrusive, or if it is a scrappy backing, choose any one of the fabrics. Sleeves should be about three to four inches wide to accommodate most quilt-show specifications. Cut a strip of fabric eight inches wide by the width of the top. It may be necessary to piece the sleeve if it is wider than 40 inches. Hem both ends and sew the strip, wrong side out, to make a long tube. Turn the tube right side out; starch and press it. Hand sew it to the top back of the quilt. Be careful not to let these stitches go through the quilt and show on the front. With a thin cotton batt, this happens often.

Hang the quilt and stand back to admire it. No matter how often you have seen it during the process, it always looks different and better with the binding sewn on and hanging nicely. Take pictures! Smile!

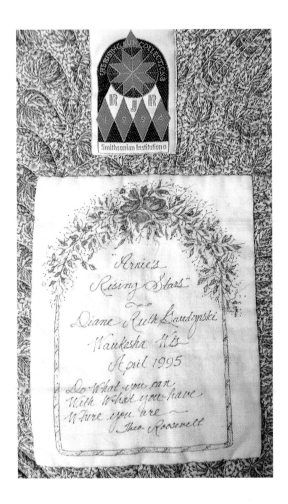

YOUR FIRST QUILT

You may have made many quilts before, but now it is time to make your first quilt using the machine quilting techniques you have just learned. Perhaps you have already machine quilted but were unhappy with the results, or maybe you wanted to try machine quilting but were too afraid you would ruin your quilt. Now is the time to designate one quilt top as a sacrifice and go ahead and quilt it for practice.

If you already machine quilt, you can change just a few of the things you have been doing, or you can jump right in and quilt a top with all the new techniques you have learned. Someone once said you have to build a house before you can build a house! That is, you learn everything you need to know about building a house by actually building one. Then you can make the next one with all the knowledge and experience you learned from that first try. It is exactly the same with quilting. Make that first quilt and learn from it. You will feel more eager than ever to use what you have learned on the next quilt and the one after that.

Practice Quilt

If you don't have a practice quilt already, you can make one. Pick a simple pattern that can be constructed quickly, such as a Nine-Patch, Irish Chain, Log Cabin, or Variable Star. Use up fabrics that maybe aren't your favorites. Make the quilt for a baby, a friend, or an in-law. They will love whatever you do, good or bad, mistakes and all.

Quilters are usually amazed when I explain that when I plan a quilt, I always consider the quilting along with the piecing from the very beginning. I think to myself how each area of the quilt will be quilted, how much quilting will be done, what kind of thread will be used, what designs will accent the style of the quilt, what "attack plan" I will use when quilting. All these things are going through my mind from the outset, and as new things come along, they are added or discarded from the general plan as I progress. You need to integrate quilting into the process from the beginning to make it easier for you when you finish the top. Quilting should become a natural fit to the quilt itself, so you don't have to say, "I couldn't think of anything else to quilt here, so I just meandered the whole thing."

While you are planning and constructing a quilt, research other quilts that are like it, with the same pattern or a similar layout. See how they are quilted. Get ideas from books, shops, quilt shows, friends, magazines. Keep a notebook for the quilt and jot down thoughts as you go along.

Practice

Use the layered practice quilt to help alleviate the anxiety of ruining your quilt. You will find that, if you know it doesn't matter if the practice piece turns out less than perfect, you will do a much better job.

But the idea that it is actually a quilt and not just a practice sandwich will give you real experience, and you will have a real quilt when you are done. It will help you rise to the occasion and do your best.

Working on a real quilt will give you the feel of what it's like to sew on something larger than a potholder. It's an entirely different process, and learning on a larger item from the first will teach you good habits.

A practice quilt provides needed repetition. If you want to learn to quilt a particular design, like a feathered wreath, first trace and quilt it on a small sample sandwich to give you an idea of how it will look, what techniques you will need, and the route you will take. After you do the sample, then proceed to your practice quilt and sew the same design every place it appears. Every time you quilt it, the results will be better. By the time you are doing the final practice wreath, you should have arrived at a new level in your quilting expertise.

The good news is that with every project you finish, your skill level will increase. If that isn't happening, then you need to go back and change some of the things that are holding you back and keep on working.

MENTAL ATTITUDE

Now that you are actually making a quilt you know will be machine quilted, your mental attitude should be changing. You will be looking at it with the idea that it is going to be sacrificed for the greater good. But you will want it to be the best you can do at this particular time, with the knowledge and experience you now have. You have to start somewhere, sometime, and your mind set should be that this quilt will lead you to greater things. Your mental attitude will shift from "I will ruin my quilt top!" to "It's nice, everyone likes it, and I know what to do on the next one. Bring it on!"

QUILTING OPTIONS

For that first machine quilting on a real quilt, keep most of the quilting at a level you know you can handle, but add a few small challenges as well. You may think you are not good enough to try a marked feather wreath, but if that's what you love, go ahead and try it. First, mark one on a practice sandwich and quilt it to see how it goes and to warm up before starting on the practice quilt.

HERE ARE SOME QUILTING IDEAS FOR THAT FIRST QUILT:

• **To stabilize the quilt,** start with in-the-ditch quilting along the seam lines between the blocks and around the borders.

• **Use continuous curves** around any triangles in the blocks or in a sawtooth border. For plain areas in alternate blocks or setting pieces, simple continuous-line designs, like a mock feather wreath, are great for beginners.

• **You can use any quilting design** that has small curvy shapes.

• **Add parallel straight lines,** done with the walking foot, in narrow borders or the final border.

• **Try some medium-sized stippling** or meandering around a design.

• **No-mark designs,** such as wavy lines, leaves, spirals, signatures, and flowers, all connected, are good for beginners.

• **Add echo quilting** to appliqué or folk-art designs.

• **Echo-quilt around the designs** in the blocks or in a border.

• **Quilt the interiors** of some shapes or echo-quilt each one once or twice to set it off.

• **You can quilt simple representational shapes,** such as leaves, cats, children's coloring book pictures, scissors, footprints, hand outlines, houses, and hearts. Just sprinkle them here and there to add interest.

• **The more quilting you do,** the more the quilt will look quilted.

Practice sandwich.

PREVENTING PAIN AND FATIGUE

"Oh my aching neck! My shoulders are killing me! I think I'm developing carpal tunnel syndrome." These are comments I hear in every class I teach. Thanks to suggestions and help from two of my quilting friends, Carol LeRoy and Carolyn Mathies, who are trained in ergonomics in the workplace, I have learned techniques to help prevent pain and fatigue while quilting.

Common Sense

The most practical and sensible people can lose sight of their own common sense when doing the thing they love. Deep down, they know they shouldn't try to finish a quilt for a deadline, but they go ahead and do it anyway, because somehow quilting overcomes common sense. It is far, far better to prevent damage than it is to fix it after it happens.

HERE ARE SOME TIPS FOR PREVENTING PAIN AND FATIGUE:

• **Limit your quilting time.** Even if you have 12 straight hours available, it's not a good idea to quilt for that length of time. Too much stress on the isolated muscles used for quilting will cause pain and will ultimately damage these areas. If it hurts, stop! Don't be stubborn and work through the pain. It will only increase the damage done and increase the time you will need to recuperate. Pain is a message from your body telling you to change something and to rest.

• **Take frequent breaks.** If you have six hours for quilting, divide it up into 20- to 30-minute periods and take at least a 15-minute break in between. The nature of the break is just as important as the break itself. Don't stop machine quilting and go to work on the computer. You will be using many of the same muscles and your eyes. Such a break would actually do more harm than good. Try to do something to oxygenate those muscles. Get up and walk around, do some stretches, load the washer, walk around the house three times, run up and down the stairs a few times, or sit in a recliner and do some deep breathing and relaxation exercises. Elevate your feet.

• **Spend some money** getting a comfortable office chair with five legs for the base for stability and with adjustable height, swivel, good lumbar support, and a seat area large enough so it doesn't put pressure on the back of your thighs and cut off circulation.

• **Remember to breathe.** When I first began machine quilting, especially stippling, I would hold my breath for long periods of time. This contributed to my feeling tired, achy, and dizzy. Concentrate on breathing. Take very deep breaths and hold them in and exhale slowly. It will relax you and get oxygen into your system so your brain can work properly, and you will be coordinated enough to machine quilt.

• **Remember to blink.** All quilting and sewing can create great strain on the eyes, especially close work. Try to keep your work about 18 inches away and have glasses, if you need them, that have a full-lens prescription rather than bifocals. You won't have to tilt your head at an awkward angle to see through the correct portion of the lens, and you won't develop neck or eye strain. Blink! Lubricate the eyes. Every half hour or so, close your eyes for a minute or two to let the muscles completely relax and the pupils dilate. Then open your eyes and focus on something across the room. Look to the left and the right, not just straight ahead. Your eyes are precious, and even though you love to quilt, taking care of them is a top priority so you will have many years of quilting fun. Be sure to have good lighting to reduce eye strain.

• **Vary your tasks.** Instead of rotary cutting all 3,000 triangles for that quilt, then sewing them all, and then pressing them all, break things up into smaller tasks to vary what you do, your body position, and the muscles used. Cut 20 triangles, or even 10, and then sew and press them. This is not a factory, this is fun! Arrange the room so you have to get up from the machine to press the piecing and then walk over to the cutting table to trim them. Changing body position and varying what you do really help prevent pain and fatigue, and you get the same amount of work done.

• **When you have to stand** for long periods at a table, put one foot up on a small foot rest. Periodically switch to the other foot.

• **Use good tools.** Look for a rotary cutter that will allow your wrist to extend naturally without having to flex it and put pressure on it. Cushion grip scissors are helpful. Look for tools that tell you they are ergonomically designed. It is worth it to replace your old ones if it will reduce or prevent pain, fatigue, and even damage to your body.

ORPHANED FEATHERED STAR, 32" x 32". A block weeded out of BUTTERNUT SUMMER provided a nice practice piece.

Part II

MACHINE-QUILTING
PROJECTS

TRIP AROUND THE WORLD WALL QUILT

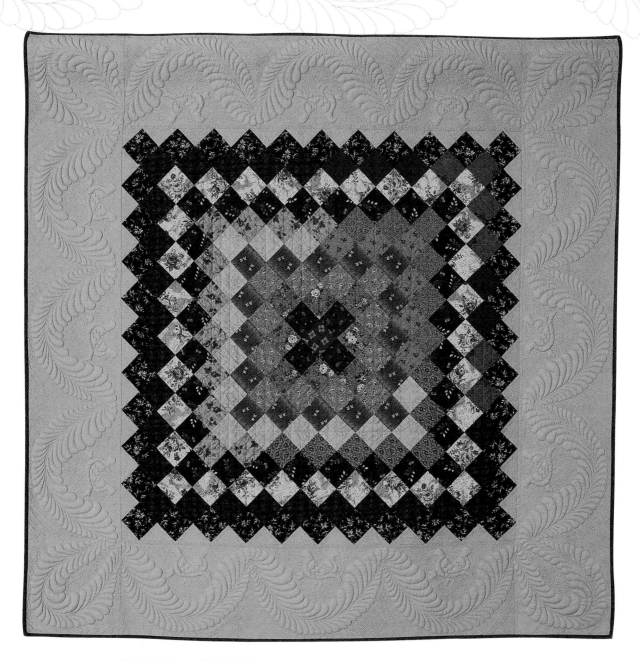

BIRDS OF A FEATHER, 50" x 50". Made by the author. Old-fashioned fabrics give this quilt a vintage flavor. (Cotton batt, trapunto, monofilament nylon thread, original feather designs. Birds by Jeanna Kimball.)

LET SLEEPING CATS LIE, 50" x 50". Made by the author. The small sleeping cats under the border feathers provided the title to this experiment in using a wool batt and silk thread. The original designs were inspired by Provence quilts.

QUILT SIZE: APPROXIMATELY 51" SQUARE
BEFORE WASHING

Fabric Requirements

You might like to read the section on Fabric Selection Tips before buying any fabrics.

Fabric	Amount
Squares	at least 11 fabrics, ranging from light to medium to very dark. The amounts will vary depending on the round. For instance, the center square can be cut from a scrap, but the outer round of squares requires ½ yd.
Border	1¾ yds.
Backing	3¼ yds.
Binding	⅝ yd.
Batting	55" x 55"

If you find color selection overwhelming, this quilt is for you. It is built in rounds from the center square outward. Take your time, put rounds up, take them down, then try something else

Use some "mud" colors, like drab brown, deep olive, khaki, chartreuse green, gold, mustard, caramel, black, olive, or moss. Then add some colors or prints you've saved for something special.

You can use muds with both pastel and dark colors. See the quilt photos for examples, but keep in mind that my preference is subdued colors with subtle contrast, soft and old-fashioned. You may prefer something more dynamic or brightly colored. Use the same concepts, but in your colorway.

Fabric Selection Tips

For an old-fashioned scrap look, use more than one fabric for each round. Decide which rounds will have more than one color or fabric. For instance, in the blue round, use two or three shades of blue, or switch to green or another color completely. Look at the photos on pages 114 and 115 to see where I have broken up a round and used several fabrics or colors.

Cut several squares from several different fabrics. Use the design wall to audition them and narrow the choices. Then, cut the number of squares needed for the design. Save the discards or give them away, but learn to use fabric as a design tool to help you build a quilt.

It's best if the border fabric is similar in color or value to one of the fabrics in the squares. The border fabric can be a solid, to show off quilting, or a print. If you prefer, you can piece the center and then choose a border fabric afterward. Sometimes that is far easier, especially if you are having problems visualizing the whole quilt.

Temporary Design Wall

For my temporary design wall, I bought about 5 yards of white baby flannel and cut it in half to make two 2½-yard lengths. The top of each panel was folded over and sewn to form a casing, as you would for a curtain. The panels were then hung on a lightweight aluminum clothes pole, the type used to hold up a sagging clothesline. The pole rests on two large nails in the studs of a wall. The flannel lengths cover the wall for designing quilts, yet they can be easily taken down and washed. The nails will also hold the pole with a quilt for photography.

Fabric Preparation

Before cutting your fabrics, wash, dry, press, and starch each one. If you have yardage, cut off and prepare only the amount you will be using for this quilt.

Cutting Instructions
SQUARES

1. Cut the following 2¾" squares for each round of fabrics:

Round	No. of squares
1 (center)	1
2	4
3	8
4	12
5	16
6	20
7	24
8	28
9	32
10	36
11 (last round)	40

SIDE TRIANGLES

2. Cut two 5" strips across the width of the border fabric. Leaving the strips folded in half once, cut off the selvages. Then make five 5" cross cuts for a total of 10 squares (Fig. 2–1).

3. Cut each square in half twice diagonally to make 40 triangles (Fig. 2–2). These triangles are sized generously and will be trimmed after the quilt is assembled.

CORNER TRIANGLES

4. From the remainder of the 5" strip of border fabric, cut two 3¼" squares. Cut each square in half once diagonally to give you four corner triangles (Fig. 2–3).

Quilt Assembly
SEWING SQUARES

5. Arrange your squares round by round. After you have arranged them to your satisfaction, make a mock-up by gluing a small scrap of each fabric to a piece of paper or cardboard in the order the fabrics go in your quilt. Use the mock-up as a guide for sewing the squares in the right sequence.

selvages   fold

Fig. 2–1. Cut 10 squares, 5" x 5", from the two strips.

Fig. 2–2. Cut each 5" square twice diagonally for the side triangles.

Fig. 2–3. Cut the two 3¼" squares in half once diagonally for the corner triangles.

Fig. 2–4. Quilt assembly.

6. Sew the squares into diagonal rows as shown in Fig. 2–4. Be sure to add the side triangles to each row. Press the seam allowances in opposite directions in alternate rows.

7. Sew the rows together. I sew the two halves separately, then sew the halves together. Press all the seam allowances between the rows in the same direction.

8. Add the four corner triangles, then press and spray-starch the quilt.

TRIMMING THE EDGES

9. Trim the four sides of the quilt by placing the ¼" ruler line of your see-through ruler on the tips of the squares that stick out the farthest (Fig. 2–5). Some of the tips may be more than ¼" in from the edge, but that's okay. They will appear to "float" in the border area, and no tips will be nipped off.

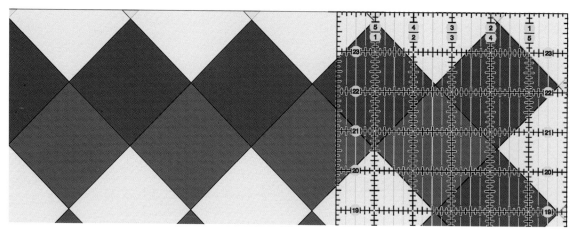

Fig. 2–5. Be sure to leave at least a ¼" seam allowance beyond each point.

10. Using a large square ruler, trim the four corners of the unit by lining up the ruler with the cut edges on adjacent sides (Fig. 2–6). The quilt should be a perfect square with a ¼" seam allowance all around.

ADDING BORDERS

11. The border measurements include an extra 2" for ensurance. Cut two border strips 8½" x 37½" and sew them to the sides of the quilt. Cut off the extra length even with the quilt's edges. Cut two border strips 8½" x 53½" and sew them to the top and bottom of the quilt. Trim off the extra length. Press well and starch.

FINISHING THE QUILT

12. Layer the quilt top, batting, and backing, then quilt the layers. Follow the instructions on page 102 for squaring the quilt. Bind the edges with seven 2"-wide bias strips sewn together end to end. Wash and block your quilt as described on pages 104–106.

QUILTING SUGGESTIONS

A simple grid works well for the squares, and you should be able to sew the grid without marking it. Just aim from one corner to the next in the rows of squares. I did the corner-to-corner lines first, then went back and aimed for a line straight down the middle between each of the already sewn lines. This way there was no marking, but my lines aren't perfectly straight either. If you really want straight lines, you can mark them.

As another option, you can quilt continuous curves around the squares. (Sewing continuous curves is described on page 78.)

The border quilting is up to you and your skill level. If you choose a print border, you can do simple quilting designs, such as fans, parallel lines, grids, overall no-mark patterns, large meanders, leaves, or loops. If you add a marked design, do some background quilting around it to finish it off.

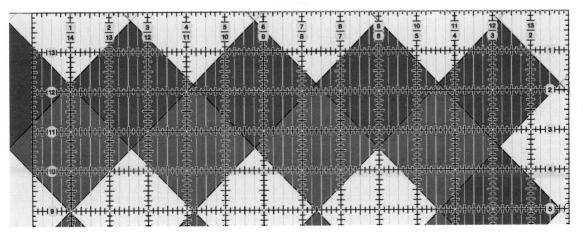

Fig. 2–6. Square up the corners. Remember to leave a seam allowance.

LOG CABIN REVISITED

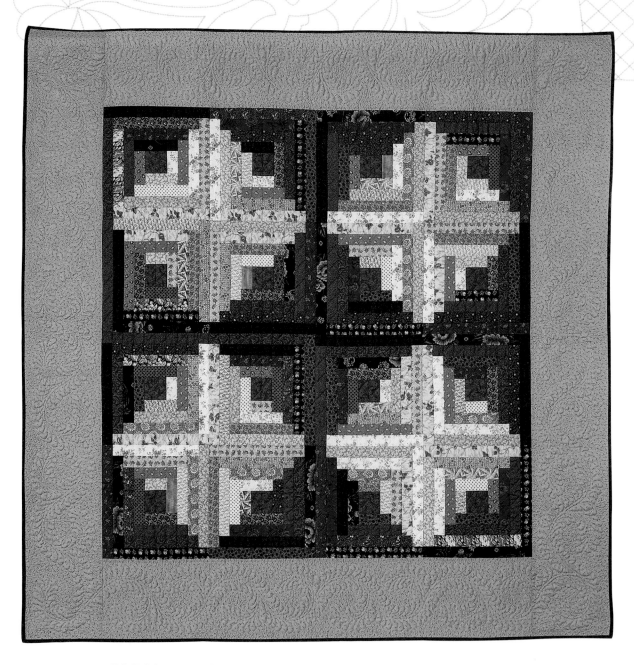

LOG CABIN, 51½" x 51½". Made by the author. Pinks and tans give this quilt a mellow, old look. (Mountain Mist cotton batt, nylon monofilament thread.)

LOG CABIN REVISITED, 86" x 86". Made by the author. Diane "sacrificed" this quilt as she learned how to use a new sewing machine. There are original trapunto quilting designs in the border.

QUILT SIZE: APPROXIMATELY 54" SQUARE
BEFORE WASHING

BLOCK SIZE: 10" FINISHED

Fabric Requirements

You might like to read the section on Fabric Selection Tips before buying any fabrics.

Fabric	Amount
Chimneys	¼ yd.
Logs	Assorted fabrics in fat quarters or ½-yd. pieces.
Border	1¾ yds.
Backing	3½ yds.
Binding	⅝ yd.
Batting	58" x 58"

Tradition tells us that the center square, called the "chimney," which is usually red, represents the hearth, the warm heart of a log cabin. The surrounding strips are the "logs," representing the cabin walls. Half the logs on one side of the cabin block are dark, and the other half are light.

This easy-to-piece quilt is made from fabric scraps. It's fun to cut many strips, pile them up, and then pick and choose each log as you experiment with color. You really can't make a color mistake if you make half the block in light fabrics and the other half in dark fabrics. Medium scraps can be mixed in on both the light and the dark sides so the quilt doesn't look so planned. When all the blocks have been completed, take some time to arrange them in various sets on a design wall to see what looks best to you.

Fabric Selection Tips

The chimneys can be cut from a solid color, or you can vary the centers by using different shades of one color or different prints of one color. If you like, you can make the centers different colors. Because the log fabrics are so scrappy, I like to unify the design by choosing a single fabric for all the centers.

You can use more than one accent fabric, such as blue and violet. Don't forget black for the dark logs. Look for a black that doesn't have white in it, for more contrast.

The binding can contrast with the border. It can be made from one of the prints used in the logs or even the chimneys.

Fabric Preparation

Before cutting your fabrics, wash, dry, press, and starch each one. If you have yardage, cut off and prepare only the amount you will use.

For instance, you can cut 12" portions from the fabric length, then cut 12" strips parallel to the selvages. This is the right length for the longest strips in the block.

Cutting Instructions

The best plan is to cut strips from each log fabric and organize them in stacks of light, medium, dark, and accent. Cut more of the fabrics you love, less of the ones you are unsure of.

1. For the chimneys, cut sixteen 2½" squares. These need to be accurate because they are the starting points for the blocks. I cut them one at a time to make sure they are precise.

2. For the logs, cut 1½" strips parallel to the selvages. This piecing method which does not require measuring and precutting the log lengths will save you time.

Piecing the Blocks

To add a log, place a strip so it extends ⅛" beyond the previous piece. Then cut the log from the strip so that the trimmed end also extends ⅛" (Fig. 2–7). After starching and pressing the unit, trim the ends even with the block (Fig. 2–8). Be sure to trim the logs consistently so the block doesn't become skewed.

3. Sew a light-colored log strip on the center square, right sides together. Cut the log from the strip as described (Fig. 2–9). Starch the unit and press it dry. Trim the ends even with square.

4. Turn the block 90 degrees to the left and add a second light strip (Fig. 2–10). Press and trim as before. Turn the unit to the left again and sew a dark strip. Turn again and add another dark strip to complete one round. Continue in this fashion until you have finished the block with four rounds (Fig. 2–11).

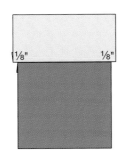

Fig. 2–7. Added logs need to extend ⅛" on both ends.

Fig. 2–8. After starching and pressing, trim logs even with the block.

Fig. 2–9. Sew a light log to the center square.

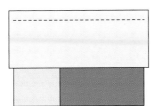

Fig. 2–10. Turn the block 90 degrees to the left and add a second light strip.

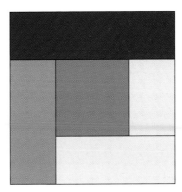

Fig. 2–11. Adding two dark strips completes the first round.

It's easy to make a mistake and sew a log on the wrong side by turning the work incorrectly or not at all. When unsure where you are in the block, count the logs out from the center. Always rotate the block in the same direction.

5. Check the block measurements to be sure the blocks are square. A small amount of trimming is okay to square up the block, or you can tug the block on the diagonal to straighten it.

Cut strips until you get a nice scrappy assortment and then piece a few blocks and see what you might need to add to the mix, then cut some more strips. Press for awhile, cut, sew, break up the tasks so you don't get tired and bored. This is a fun quilt to make with a friend too because there is no thinking needed, and you can get in a lot of talking.

At the Design Wall

As I make the blocks, instead of stacking them up and putting them aside, I place them on my design wall. That way, I can see exactly how the quilt is progressing at a glance and know immediately if the fabrics I have chosen are working. Using the design wall like this helps me pick strips for each block and makes the final assembly much easier. There is always room for rearranging blocks as well or removing some if they don't work. A design wall also provides a nice out-of-the way storage place for the blocks as they are being pieced.

Quilt Assembly
SEWING THE ROWS

6. Pin the blocks together in rows, making sure the log seamlines align. Sometimes you may have to trim or ease the blocks a bit to make them fit. Sew the blocks in each row together (Fig. 2–12). Press the seam allowances in each row in opposite directions.

7. Sew the rows together. I usually sew the two halves of the quilt and then sew the halves together. Pin carefully, easing if necessary. Thorough, careful pinning saves time in the long run. Press the row seam allowances all in one direction, up or down. When all sewn together, your quilt should be flat, square, and stiff from starch. Don't worry. It comes out when you wash it.

ADDING BORDERS

8. The cut borders are extra long for ensurance. Cut two border strips 7½" x 42½" and sew them to the sides of the quilt. Cut off the extra length even with the quilt's edges. Cut two border strips 7½" x 56½" and sew them to the top and bottom of the quilt. Trim off the extra length. Press well and starch.

FINISHING THE QUILT

9. Layer the quilt top, batting, and backing, then quilt the layers. Follow the instructions on page 102 for squaring the quilt. Bind the edges with seven 2"-wide bias strips sewn together end to end. Wash and block your quilt.

QUILTING SUGGESTIONS

The blocks were quilted with a hanging-diamond grid. The measured and marked diagonal lines are 1" apart. The vertical lines were sewn by using the seam lines as guides. Portions of the vertical lines were marked.

The border provides an area for some quilting designs, with background quilting or an overall design like fans or clamshells. Stippling in the background will flatten the borders nicely so the quilt will hang straight.

Fig. 2–12. Quilt assembly.

BASKET QUILT

SIXTEEN BASKETS OF MUD, 56½" x 56½". Made by the author. This quilt was made in response to a challenge to herself to use only "fabric on hand."

ODE TO DIANE, 49" x 49". Made by Joan Zeier Poole. This quilt was worked on in a class with Diane. Joan created the quilting designs. ODE TO DIANE won first place in the large wall quilt category at the 2000 Prairie Heritage Quilt Show in Sun Prairie, Wisconsin. PHOTO: NORMAN LENBURG

QUILT SIZE: APPROXIMATELY 58" SQUARE
BEFORE WASHING

BLOCK SIZE: 7½" FINISHED

Fabric Requirements

You might like to read the section on Fabric Selection Tips before buying any fabrics.

Fabric	Yards	Cutting
Basket triangles (foundation piecing)	scraps	56 squares 3"
Basket body	½	32 A, 16 B
Handles	½	16 bias strips
Background	⅞	16 C, 32 D, 16 E
Sashing	½	24 rectangles 2½" x 8"
Cornerstones	⅛	9 squares 2½"
*Inner border	1½	2 strips 2½" x 42½" 2 strips 2½" x 38½"
Sawtooth border	scraps	42 squares 2⅞"
Outer border	2	2 strips 7½" x 60½", 2 strips 7½" x 46½", 42 squares 2⅞"
Backing	3⅝	2 panels 32" x 62"
Binding	⅝	—
Batting	—	62" x 62"

* Your inner border width may differ (see Adding borders, page 131).

Most quilts have stories behind them, and this unassuming little quilt has had quite a journey from my first sketch to winning a first-place award at the 1998 American Quilter's Society Show in Paducah, Kentucky. It started out as a reward I promised myself in 1996 when I bought my first computer. I had to spend many frustrating hours closeted with this machine, trying desperately to learn its little electronic ways. To make the hours more pleasant, I bought a big framed print of an old basket quilt made of washed-out everyday shirtings and calicoes, set with homespun squares, and quilted in a simple pattern. Only a few livelier fabrics were used here and there in the small triangles in the baskets. These were obviously the quilter's treasured "pretty" fabrics, hoarded and parceled out sparingly to give the quilt its charm. I promised myself that, if and when I learned this new-fangled computer contraption, I would draft that basket block and make a small quilt, similar to the one in the photo, by using only what I had on hand. When I made my quilt, I added sashing and several borders, but the essential idea of the old quilt has been captured in SIXTEEN BASKETS OF MUD.

Fabric Selection Tips

You will need a great variety of fabrics but not much of each one. Fat quarters are great for the triangles, the baskets, or even the block backgrounds. The scrappier the quilt, the better. You may have to piece some scraps together to get a piece large enough for a particular patch, but go ahead.

That is exactly what the maker of the original quilt would have done.

The one splash of color in this quilt is in the sashing fabric. It can be a repeat of one of the colors used in the basket triangles or something completely different. The basket backgrounds and the borders are done in neutral colors, so the sashing and cornerstones take on quite a bit of importance and can change the entire look of the quilt.

To test possible sashing choices, cut 2½" strips of various fabrics and place them between the blocks. Alternatively, you can hang a whole piece of sashing fabric on the wall and pin the blocks to it, leaving the right amount of space between blocks to show through as sashing.

The sawtooth border is made up of scrappy triangles pieced with triangles cut from the outer border fabric. The scraps are arranged randomly, as if they had been taken directly from a scrap bag rather than carefully arranged around the edges of the quilt.

Fabric Preparation

Before cutting your fabrics, wash, dry, press, and starch each one. (Use heavy starch for the background fabric.) If you have yardage, cut off and prepare only the amount you will use.

Making a Prototype Block

A good rule of thumb, when beginning any project, is to cut pieces for one block, then sew a block as a prototype. Check the sizing, seam allowance width, etc., in the prototype and use it as a guide for making the actual quilt blocks. Take notes as you make the block. I have heard too many sad stories from students who cut all the pieces for an entire quilt, only to find it would have worked so much better in a slightly altered size, or perhaps there was a mistake in the directions. Plan ahead!

To make a prototype, refer to Fig. 2–13 and the quilt photo. Cut four oversized foundation triangles from one fabric and three from another. Using the patterns on pages 133–135, foundation piece the triangles. From the appropriate fabrics, cut one each of patches B, C, and F. Cut two each of patches D and E. Sew the prototype block and check it.

Block Construction

1. If the prototype block is satisfactory, cut the pieces listed in the Fabric Requirements chart and make the basket portion for each of the 16 blocks (Fig. 2–14, page 130). Starch, press, and trim the half blocks.

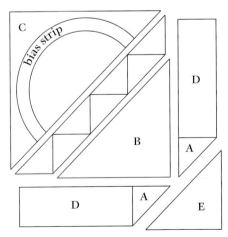

Fig. 2–13. Block assembly.

2. Fold each bias handle strip in half lengthwise, wrong sides together, and sew along the long edges with a ¼" seam allowance. Trim the seam allowance to ⅛".

3. Insert a pressing bar in the tube and center the seam on the back (Fig. 2–15). Press the side with the seam first, then press the other side. Remove bar and press the handle with spray starch.

4. Lightly trace the inner edge of the handles on the C triangles. Position the handle along the line, bending, stretching, and tweaking it to make a smooth, even curve. There is some overhang at each end which will be trimmed later.

5. Using a fabric glue stick or basting stitches, place the handle on the background triangle. Appliqué the inner curve of the handle first, then the outer curve. If you prefer, you can topstitch the handle to the background. Trim off the overhang even with the triangle's edge (Fig. 2–16).

6. Sew the two halves of the blocks together, checking to make sure the basket handles are centered over the row of triangles. Press the seam allowances either toward the basket or open, whichever works best for you. Spray starch and press lightly from top.

7. Using a large square ruler and the sides of the blocks as guidelines, square up the blocks to an even 8", which includes seam allowances.

Because the handle half of the block may be distorted by the appliqué, square up the basket half first. Be careful not to trim too close to the handles. There should be enough fabric left for the seam allowance and some space between the handle and the block seam.

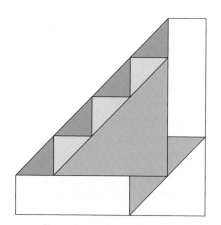

Fig. 2–14. Start by making the basket portions of the blocks.

Fig. 2–15. Center the seam line on the back of the pressing bar.

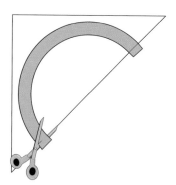

Fig. 2–16. Trim off the overhang.

Quilt Assembly

8. Place the blocks on your design wall or other flat surface and arrange them to your liking (Fig. 2–17). If the blocks seem to need something, now is the time to replace blocks and add a touch of a new color. Remember, though, it is the sashing color that adds brightness to the baskets.

9. Sew sashing strips between the blocks in each row. Lightly spray starch the rows and press the seam allowances toward the sashing.

10. Sew four sashing strips and three cornerstones together to make a sashing row. Starch and press the allowances toward the sashing

11. Sew the block rows and sashing rows together as shown in the quilt assembly diagram.

Adding Borders

12. The inner and outer borders are cut extra long to allow for a custom fit. For the inner border, sew the 38½" strips to two opposite sides of the quilt. Trim the ends even with the quilt's edge. Then sew the 42½" strips to the remaining sides and trim as before. Your quilt should now measure 40½" by 40½". If it doesn't, you will need to adjust the width of the inner border until it does, so the sawtooth border will fit. The width of the inner border can be changed as needed to facilitate fitting a pieced border to a quilt body. An inner border used in this way is called a spacer strip.

13. For the sawtooth border, cut all the 2⅞" squares in half diagonally. Pair the scrap triangles with the border-fabric triangles to make 84 half-squares (Fig. 2–18). The units need to measure 2½" for the border to fit correctly. Trim or resew the units as needed for the correct measurement.

14. Arrange the half-squares around the quilt. Chain sew each border in pairs, then join the pairs in units of four, then eight, etc., until 20 units have been sewn together (Fig. 2–19, page 132). Make four of these

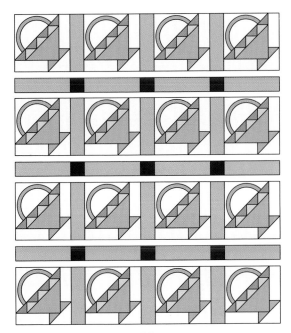

Fig. 2–17. Quilt assembly.

Fig. 2–18. Sawtooth border unit.

border strips. Spray starch and press the seams from the top. Check for fit on the quilt, and if you need to make any adjustments, you can do it at this point.

15. Using the quilt photo as a guide for orienting the triangles, sew on the two side borders. Add a half-square to each end of the remaining border strips and sew them to the top and bottom of the quilt.

16. For the outer border, sew the 46½" strips to two opposite sides of the quilt. Trim the ends even with the quilt's edge. Then sew the 60½" strips to the remaining sides and trim as before.

FINISHING THE QUILT

17. Layer the quilt top, batting, and backing, then quilt the layers. Follow the instructions on page 102 for squaring the quilt. Bind the edges with seven 2"-wide bias strips sewn together end to end. Wash and block your quilt as described on pages 104–106.

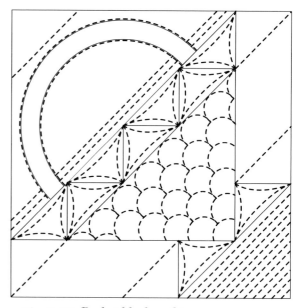

Fig. 2–20. Basket block quilting.

QUILTING SUGGESTIONS

Stitch-in-the-ditch quilting was done between all the sashing pieces, blocks, and borders to stabilize the quilt. A small cable was used in the sashing with an "X" in the cornerstones. Continuous curves were quilted in the sawtooth triangles and in the triangles in the basket. Clamshells were added in the baskets (Fig. 2–20).

Parallel straight lines, ¼" apart, were quilted in the background of each basket. They were not marked. A feather stencil was used for the border, which includes stippling. There was no corner design, so each corner looks a bit different, adding to the whimsy of this quilt. The inner border was quilted along the stripes.

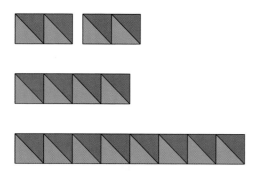

Fig. 2–19. Border strip

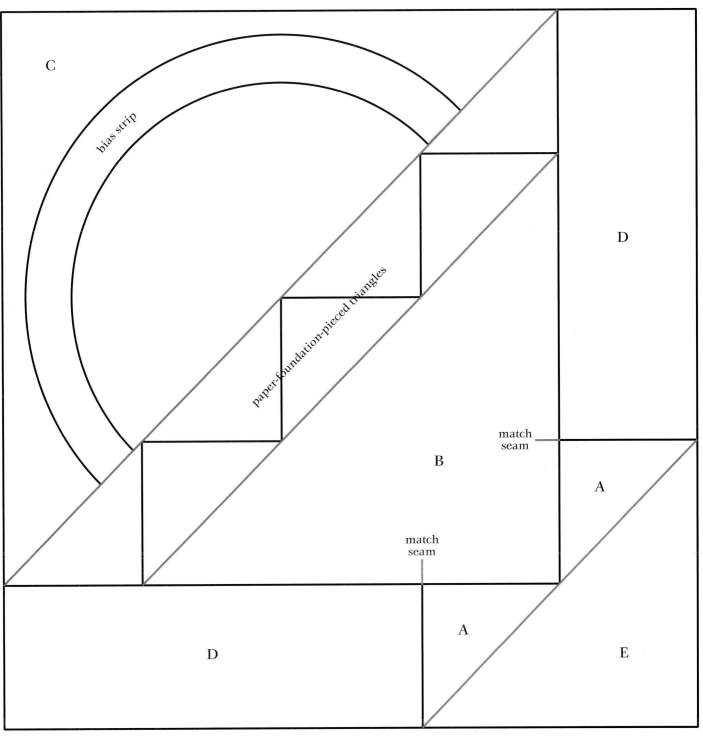

Use this full-sized guide to check your units as you sew the block, especially the placement of the seam line between A and D relative to B.

The A triangles are cut oversized. To sew an A to a D, match the edges on the side to be sewn to B. (The tip of triangle A will extend beyond B toward the outside of the block.) Sew both A/D units to B. Then trim the the A's along the side to be sewn to E. Be sure to leave a ¼" seam allowance beyond the tip of the B triangle.

Background triangles C and E are also cut oversized. They will be trimmed when the block is squared to 8".

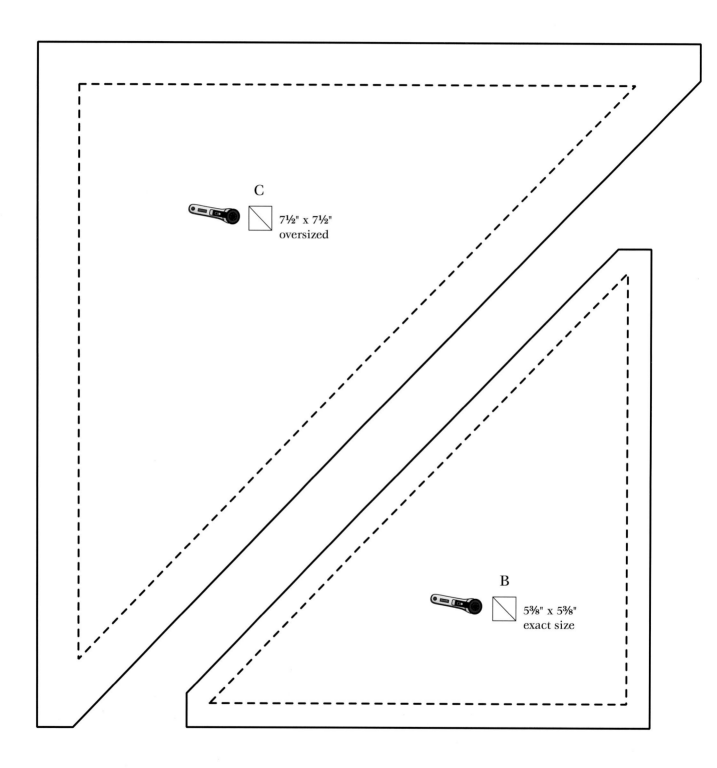

C
7½" x 7½"
oversized

B
5⅜" x 5⅜"
exact size

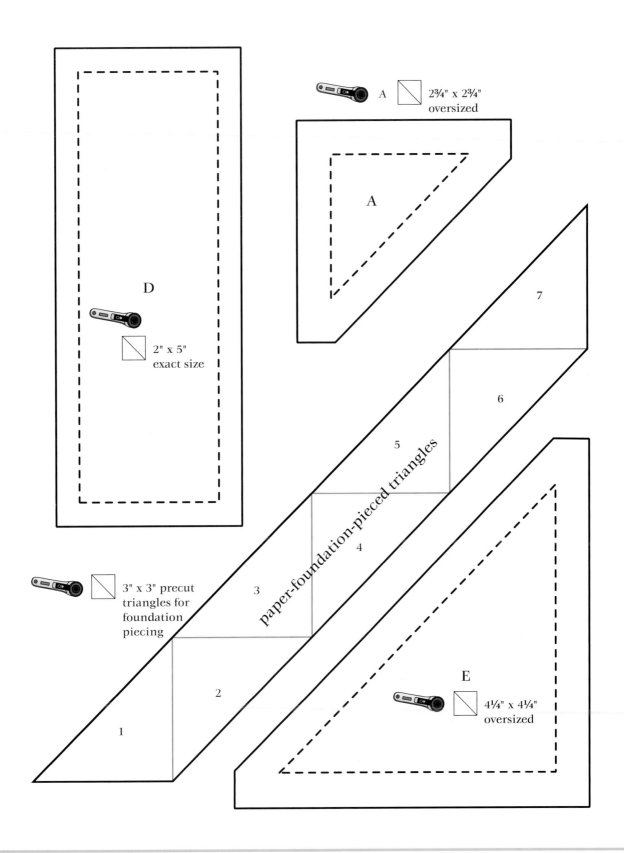

A 2¾" x 2¾" oversized

A

D

2" x 5" exact size

7

6

5

paper-foundation-pieced triangles

4

3

3" x 3" precut triangles for foundation piecing

2

1

E 4¼" x 4¼" oversized

Quilting Samples

Class Sample, 15½" x 15½". Made by the author. (Wholecloth stencil, cotton sateen, taupe silk thread, Quilter's Dream cotton batt.)

Class sample, 15½" x 15½". Made by the author. (Chintz fabric, Cotton Classic batt, trapunto, clear nylon monofilament thread.)

ABOVE: **LEAFY GREENS.** Made by the author. (Hand-dyed fabric, cotton batt, trapunto, taupe silk thread; original design.)

LEFT: Class sample, 18" x 18". Made by the author. (Combination of several stencils and backgrounds, cotton batt, trapunto, nylon monofilament thread.)

ABOVE: **FEATHER MY VEST.** Made by the author. This vest was made in a rush to wear to the AQS Show in 2000. (Original design, hand-dyed fabric, silk thread, trapunto.)

RIGHT: Class sample, 17" x 19". Made by the author. (Wholecloth stencil, Hobbs 100% cotton batt, silk thread.)

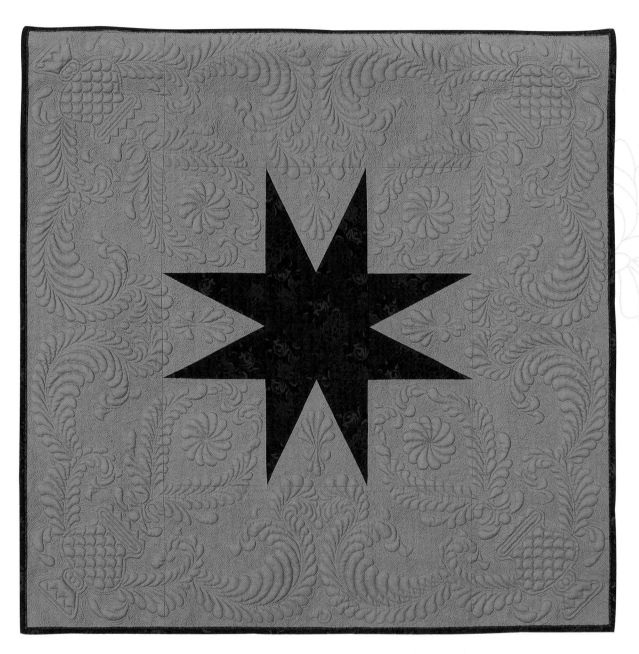

ROSES IN BLUE, 38" x 38". Made by the author. Inspired by a very large antique star quilt, Diane made ROSES IN BLUE for her brother Neil Hinterberg. The trapunto designs are based on Rose Kretsinger's stylized feathers. This quilt is featured on the cover.

BIBLIOGRAPHY

Aug, Bobbie A., and Sharon Newman. *Vertical Quilts With Style.* American Quilter's Society, Paducah, KY, 2000.

Beyer, Jinny. *Color Confidence for Quilters.* Quilt Digest Press, Lincolnwood, IL, 1992.

Cory, Pepper. *Mastering Quilt Marking.* C & T Publishing, Lafayette, CA, 1999.

Cross, Mary Bywater. *Quilts & Women of the Mormon Migrations.* Rutledge Hill Press, Nashville, TN, 1996.

Fons, Marianne, and Liz Porter. *Quilter's Complete Guide.* Oxmoor House and Leisure Arts, Birmingham, AL, 1993.

Gordon, Maggi McCormick. *The Ultimate Quilting Book.* Collins & Brown, New York, 1999.

Hall, Carrie A., and Rose G. Kretsinger. *The Romance of the Patchwork Quilt.* Dover Publications, Mineola, NY, 1935, 1988.

Hargrave, Harriet. *Heirloom Machine Quilting.* C & T Publishing, Lafayette, CA, 1995.

Hargrave, Harriet. *From Fiber to Fabric.* C & T Publishing, Lafayette, CA, 1997.

Lipsett, Linda Otto. *Remember Me – Women and Their Friendship Quilts.* Quilt Digest Press, Lincolnwood, IL, 1997, 1985.

Marston, Gwen, and Joe Cunningham. *Quilting With Style.* American Quilter's Society, Paducah, KY, 1993.

McCloskey, Marsha. *Feathered Star Quilts.* Feathered Star Productions, Seattle, WA, 1987.

Nelson, Cyril I., and Carter Houck. *Treasury of American Quilts.* Wings Books, Avenel, NJ, 1982.

Noble, Maurine. *Machine Quilting Made Easy.* That Patchwork Place, Bothell, WA, 1994.

Oliver, Celia Y. *Enduring Grace – Quilts from the Shelburne Museum Collection.* C & T Publishing, Lafayette, CA, 1997.

Pilgrim, Paul D., and Gerald E. Roy. *The Log Cabin Returns to Kentucky.* American Quilter's Society, Paducah, KY, 1992.

Rae, Janet, et al. *Quilt Treasures of Great Britain.* Rutledge Hill Press, Nashville, TN, 1995.

Ramsey, Bets, and Merikay Waldvogel. *Southern Quilts – Surviving Relics of the Civil War.* Rutledge Hill Press, Nashville, TN, 1998.

Safford, Carleton L., and Robert Bishop. *America's Quilts and Coverlets.* E.P. Dutton, New York, 1972.

Shackelford, Anita. *Surface Textures.* American Quilter's Society, Paducah, KY, 1997.

Squire, Helen. *Helen's Guide to Quilting in the 21st Century.* American Quilter's Society, Paducah, KY, 1996.

Stori, Mary. *The Wholecloth Garment Stori.* American Quilter's Society, Paducah, KY, 1998.

Thompson, Shirley. *Think Small.* Powell Publications, Edmonds, WA, 1990.

Walner, Hari. *Trapunto by Machine.* C & T Publishing, Lafayette, CA, 1996.

ABOUT THE AUTHOR

Having slept under her grandmother's hand-quilted scrap quilts when she was a child, author Diane Gaudynski has loved quilts her entire life. However, she didn't learn how to do hand quilting until 1978. Then in 1988, she began machine quilting. A self-taught machine quilter, Diane makes traditional-style, everyday quilts with "Sunday best" quilting. Her style reflects her love of drab "mud" colors and simple elegant design inspired by antique quilts.

Living in Waukesha, Wisconsin, with her husband and four cats, she finds the long, cold winters great for serious quiltmaking. An experienced teacher and lecturer, Diane loves to encourage beginners so they too can sleep under beautiful quilts.

The author has had nine quilts juried into the American Quilter's Society show in Paducah, Kentucky. Four of them won the Bernina Award for Machine Workmanship, and they are now part of the permanent collection of the Museum of the American Quilter's Society. She also received the Pfaff Master Award for Machine Artistry in 2001.

She has written several magazine articles and has appeared on the PBS documentary "America Quilts" and "Quilt Central." In 2002, Diane's work was included in an international exhibit in Tokyo, Japan, called Thirty Distinguished Quilt Artists of the World. Her quilt THROUGH A GLASS DARKLY: AN AMERICAN MEMORY was judged a Masterpiece Quilt by NQA in 2002. You can visit Diane at her website.

< http://personal.pitnet.net/dgquilt >

OTHER AQS Books

This is only a small selection of the books available from the American Quilter's Society. AQS books are known worldwide for timely topics, clear writing, beautiful color photos, and accurate illustrations and patterns. The following books are available from your local bookseller, quilt shop, or public library.

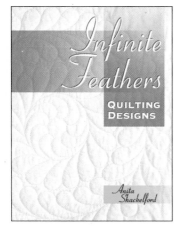

#6072   us$25.95

#6079   us$21.95

#5855   us$22.95

#6000   us$24.95

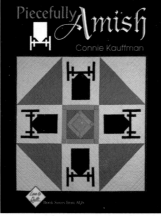

#6003   us$16.95

#6006   us$25.95

#6073   us$19.95

#6071   us$22.95

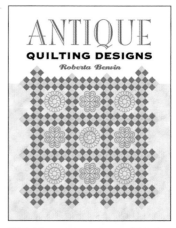

#5849   us$21.95